Dynamic Fund Raising Projects

Second Edition

by

Rick Montana

Printed by CreateSpace

Second edition revised and updated

Copyright © 2016 by Rick Arledge

All rights reserved.

No part of this book may be reproduced, scanned, or distributed in any printed or electronic form without permission.

ISBN-10: 1535526297

ISBN-13: 978-1535526296

About the Author

Rick Montana wrote the original "Dynamic Fund Raising Projects" in 1990. With so many changes in technology and the way we do business in this millennium, the old book was very dated and begged for a rewrite. During his action packed lifetime, Rick has worked in professional wrestling, fair promotions, tough man boxing, concert promotions, local television, and even a number of TV movies. He also squeezed in a career in government service working for the Army, Air Force, and with the Navy. He retired from his position as Director of the National Advertising Division for the U.S. Navy in 2013. In that position he was responsible for all national advertising in support of Navy recruiting to include production of TV commercials, recruiting videos, social media, Navy.com, print media, and direct mail campaigns. With all that to keep him busy, he still managed to work with the Jaycees, American Legion, volunteer fire departments, schools, and other service clubs to help them with their fund raising efforts. That is where he got the idea for this book.

Rick Montana has earned an Associates of Applied Science Degree in Electronic Technology, Bachelor of Science Degree in Psychology and Business, and a Master of Science Degree in Counseling. He is a lifetime member of the Alabama Jaycees, the American Legion, and a past member of the Professional Marketing Association, the Screen Actors Guild, and the International Independent Showman's Association.

Also by Rick Montana

An Alien View of Human History

Straight Talk: Unintended Consequences

Straight Talk: Political Correctness

Zombie Ranger: A New Beginning

TABLE OF CONTENTS

	Page
How to Use This Book	1
Sixteen Steps to Success	4
Generic 300 Club	14
Rummage Sales	24
Direct Mail Campaigns	30
Fairs and Carnivals	35
Haunted Houses	46
Custom T-Shirt Sales	53
Concession Stands	58
Automobile Party	66
Concert Promotions	76
Movie Premieres	84
Auctions	89
Professional Wrestling	96
Pancake Breakfast	104
Resource List	110
Carnival Supplies	111
Custom T-Shirt Printing	113
Poster Printing	114
Event Insurance	115
Professional Wrestling Organizations	115
Concert Info	116

HOW TO USE THIS BOOK

The purpose of this book is to aid you and the organizations you serve. All the fund raising ideas covered in this book have been tested and found to be **workable and profitable**. Simply follow the step by step instructions provided to assure the success of your fund raising endeavor.

We'll begin with ideas which may be implemented with little or no investment. Each of these ideas will generate from hundreds to thousands of dollars depending on the scale of application. You **choose the amount of money that you need** to generate and apply these well tested ideas to that end.

Some of the ideas with the most profit potential also entail greater risk. Common sense tells us that this is always the case, yet there are exceptions, as you will see. For example, the **Generic 300 Club** should generate a **net profit of more than one third of gross income**, yet requires a very small initial investment. In its most common form, this means that with projected gross income of $15,000, there should be a profit of at least $5,000. After I explain the mechanics of the Generic 300 Club you will see how this is possible.

The **Automobile Party** is an example of a high risk/high return venture. If successful, it **should yield a net profit of about $10,000**. On the other hand, it can also lose your organization up to $20,000 if unsuccessful. In the section covering automobile parties I will describe the steps which will add to your success and point out some of the potential problems to avoid.

I do not claim to have invented these ideas or guarantee in any way that you will be successful in using them. I do guarantee that all of them have been used successfully in the past by a wide range of groups and organizations. Ultimately, your success or failure depends on the amount of work your members put into implementation of the ideas outlined in the following sections. By providing these ideas in one source book, I will help you to **choose a fund raising vehicle that will work in your unique situation**. Nothing is worse than working on a fund raising project only to discover that you overlooked a critical ingredient during your planning stages. By following the program outline for your choice of the ideas presented, you virtually eliminate the chance of making a serious mistake during the planning of your fund raising event.

As you probably have guessed, I have been involved in or observed each of these projects first hand. For example, one of the civic groups I belong to had fallen on hard times. They owned their own club house free and clear but could no longer afford to pay their utilities on time. They had small bills around town for advertising, food, entertainment, trophies, plaques, and so on that they were unable to pay. They borrowed money against a certificate of deposit that the organization had held for over ten years. They usually passed the hat among the membership in order to make payments on the debt. Yes, things were getting desperate. I knew the club's glorious history of service in the local community and did not want to see them fold up. True, times were hard, but I felt that a new approach could get them back on track. You see, they relied almost exclusively on contributions and had forgotten how to actually **earn money from their projects**. I have seen many clubs just stand on the street with a bucket and try to guilt people into contributing. I believe that sets a bad precedent and perpetuates the wrong ideals. My personal belief is that the fund raising projects outlined in this book can do three important things for your organization.

First, they will **earn the money your organization requires to operate and do good things** for your community.

Second, these projects provide something to the community at the same time that you are earning the money your organization needs to survive. You are not just asking for a hand-out. You are **providing an exciting event or community service in return for financial support**.

Third, your **members learn by doing as they perform these fund raising projects**. For the future of your community, this may be the best reason of all. Success breeds success. When your members experience the great feeling of running a successful project, they will be excited and tell everyone they know about how great it is to be a member of your organization. A club that runs highly visible projects in the community will grow because people want to be part of a successful organization.

Back to the dire financial straits I found my club in. Since their backs were to the wall and they really had no choice, they accepted my advice to change directions in their fund raising efforts. The **main obstacle to overcome was inertia**. Most clubs become stagnant in their approach to fund raising and **do the same thing year after year**. It has now been many years since we had to pass the hat to pay bills. All the club's **debts were paid**. The **clubhouse was remodeled**. The club **purchased a piece of investment property** to be used as a permanent location for their annual Haunted House project. All their projects were bigger and better than ever. Because of the success of all these projects, **membership also grew**.

Please remember: **Not all of these projects are right for your organization**. However, I promise that **some of them are right for you and you can make money with them** if you follow the steps outlined in the following chapters. These projects range from those requiring little or no up-front investment to those in which your club must risk thousands of dollars. Each project is **designed to fit a specific set of needs**. With so many fund raising projects outlined, you can **choose the amount of money that you need to generate, the risk you are prepared to take, and match it to the appropriate project**.

I decided to write the first edition of this book on fund raising in 1990 because I saw civic groups make the **same mistakes year after year**. Now that another twenty-five years have passed, it was time for an update. The very nature of most volunteer organizations, with their high membership turn-over and resistance to change, created a need for a source document on fund raising. My dream was that this book will be a permanent part of every club. That it will be used for years to come **to help your organization reach its financial goals**. I've seen the dynamic results achieved from these projects and their effects on the local community. I want to **spread the word** so that you can quit wasting time re-inventing the wheel. You should spend that time doing better things for your local community. I want to help **restore the pride in America** that infused civic groups across the nation as they worked to make their community a better place to live. By helping you **solve the riddle of how to raise money** for your organization, I hope to be **part our return to greatness**.

Rick Montana

SIXTEEN STEPS TO SUCCESS

There are certain steps you should take to determine if you should go ahead with your plans for a fund raising event. Not all of them apply to every project. This is designed to be a general guide which will keep you from making plans for an event that is doomed to failure from the start. Pick an event and then use the steps that apply to your project.

1. **Form a committee**. The members of your committee will either make your event a success or cause it to fail. I cannot stress enough the importance of forming a good committee. Do not try to do everything yourself. Take advantage of the strengths of each of your committee members. If you have a member who works at a radio station or newspaper, appoint that person publicity chairman. If a member works at an automobile dealership, make that member the prize chairman for your automobile party. Recognize the specialized skills that each member of your committee brings to the table and take advantage of them.

2. **Select a tentative date for your event**. The date must be tentative because you may not be able to stage your event on your first choice. Do some research to determine whether your local community supports events better on weekends or midweek. I have staged events in one town that will only be supported if presented on a weeknight. In another town, less than fifteen miles away, you will only draw a crowd for an event that is held on Saturday night. You must do your research and know what works best in your local area.

3. **Find out what else is planned for the date of your event**. I have seen events unrelated to football planned during the Super Bowl. Needless to say, they did not fare too well. Other local events can have just as severe an impact on your ability to raise money. Do your best to be the only game in town on the date of your event. In one local community, two different groups scheduled a performance of the Temptations as a fund raiser on the same night! Each group had one of the original members of the Temptations, but both groups used the name. You can imagine how that turned out. Another group scheduled a full-fledged fair without knowing that a parking lot carnival was playing in town the same week. A little research would have kept this from happening. You have to do your homework!

4. **Check to see if a similar event has been staged recently**. You want to have a unique event. Chances are that you will lose money if you schedule a circus within a few weeks of another circus in your town. This is especially true for events like the Automobile Party. You have to sell 300 tickets for $100 each to make it a success. Most local economies will not support more than one Automobile Party in the same year. The same rule applies to all types of fund raising events. You want your project to be seen as unique. Failure to follow this guideline can be a very costly mistake but one that is easily avoided.

5. **Determine if there is community interest and support for your event**. This is difficult to do. The best way is to compare your event to other successful events that have been held in your community. Are they similar? Does your event seem to appeal to the same audience? See what has worked and what hasn't. If a group puts on a successful concert, you should try to isolate what made it successful. Was it because of the type of music played? Was it the ticket price that made people turn out? Was it where the concert was held? You get the picture. Never assume that just because you like something, everybody else will. Talk to a lot of people and ask direct questions. Don't just ask if they think your event is a good idea. Ask people if they will spend their money and attend your event. Many people will tell you that you have a good idea because they don't want to hurt your feelings. It's quite another thing for them to pay to attend your event.

6. **Select an event and stay with it**. After you have gone through the first five steps you'll have a good idea of what will work in your community. You must have faith in the profit generating potential of your event and not stray from your proven concept. Make notes to improve next year's event, but don't keep making changes as you go along until your event is changed beyond recognition. After analyzing the needs of the local community, I started a county fair for the Jaycees. It ran for over 20 years and generated a profit every year. Each year I spent less and less on advertising because the community expected the fair to magically appear in September. The momentum gained by building up community expectations cannot be stressed enough.

7. **Develop a goal**. Decide what you want to accomplish both monetarily and in the form of service to the community. Be realistic. Many times I have seen civic groups set unachievable goals and then worry themselves to death over their failure to accomplish those goals. If you need to make about $5,000 with low risk, try

something like the Generic 300 Club. If you have plenty of working capital, you could try an automobile party. The automobile party could net about $10,000 if fully successful. Your goal may be simply to entertain the community and break even. That is a worthy goal. Not every project has to produce a surplus. All you must do is establish what your goal is, and then strive to achieve it.

8. **Make a budget**. A budget should be used as a road map to reaching your goal. The quickest way I know to let your money slip away is to stage an event without a budget. The entire committee must take an active role in planning the budget. Generally speaking, no single individual should attempt to develop a budget for your event. Use the expertise of your committee members to establish reasonable costs and income objectives. Some clubs will be lucky enough to have a member with extensive experience in planning and presenting events. If so, listen to that person. I recently saw an organization presenting a Haunted House. They apparently listened to the person with the loudest voice, not the most experience. The loud voice insisted that the Haunted House was in a good enough location that any advertising expense would just be wasted money. All the other civic groups in the area spent money on radio advertising. The end result was that revenue from this Haunted House was down about $3,000 from the prior year when they spent a few hundred dollars on radio advertising. Remember that your civic organization can usually get a discount or sometimes a little free advertising when they have a good cause they are supporting. Don't be penny wise and pound foolish. It will cost you money!

9. **Determine how many people it will take to stage your event and where you will get them.** Every organization has "paper members." These are members that are on the rolls, pay their dues, and rarely participate in club projects. You have to make a realistic assessment of whether you have enough dedicated club members to put on your project. Your first step is to determine how many people it will take to put on your planned event. Once you have that number in hand, then you must figure out where to get them. Just because you don't have enough members doesn't automatically rule out a project.

Events like fairs lend themselves to cooperative ventures with other clubs. Maybe you want to have another club operate the parking lot and split the revenue with your club. The main thing to watch for in cooperative ventures is that the club that gets "first count" generally makes the most money. That means if an outside organization runs your parking lot and handles the money, you will probably get a smaller share than you think you will. That goes for anything you let someone else run. Sometimes it's better to accept a flat rate from them than it is to worry about how much they are stealing from you. This may sound cynical but years of experience taught me this!

Never assume that people are honest. Many people who are normally honest will be tempted to put something in their pocket when they see a large amount of cash coming in. Somehow they rationalize that if you don't know it exists, you won't miss it. Another way you can get hurt quickly is when people are allowed to come into your event for free. Volunteers often think that they should be allowed to bring in family and friends for free since they are not being paid to help. I have found that it is much cheaper to pay the people who handle your money than it is to use volunteers.

Determine which jobs are really critical and pay people to do them rather than rely on volunteers. At one fair I ran, volunteers were supposed to walk along the fence to deter people from getting in free. On the first Saturday night, the busiest time of the fair, no volunteers showed up to police the fence line. In the first two hours I estimated that over 200 people sneaked in. At $7 per person, that represents $1,400 in lost revenue. After that, I always hired two people with flashlights to guard the fence. In their first hour on the job, they directed over 100 people to the front gate where they each paid to get in. A couple of minimum wage employees saved us about $700 in one hour.

Any time you run a successful event you must watch out for outside organizations that see how well you did on your event and try to take it over. That happens more often than you think. People can always convince themselves that they can do the event better than you can so it's good for the community if they take over.

10. **Advertise, advertise, and then advertise some more**. Just because your membership and their friends know about your event, that does not mean that everyone in town knows about it. It is easy to think that word of mouth alone is all you need. It certainly helps, but word of mouth alone will not achieve the results you want. Any event geared to an audience under 50 years of age should be advertised on the radio. Even then, not just any radio station will do.

One civic group I worked with always used radio to spread the news about their events but still had low attendance. I asked them how they chose the station they advertised on? They replied that the advertising rates were low and the owner had been a member of the club about 20 years ago! The station was AM radio, and aimed at the elderly, shut-in market. It was basically a call-in talk show format. Lonely shut-ins would call in and complain about something and then others would call in to respond. The station had the lowest market share in the local community. No wonder the rates were cheap!

Picking the right radio station to advertise on can be really difficult. In the old days, there might only be one station in town (and it was locally owned) so it was easy to choose where to advertise. Today there are so many niche stations that advertising on one that hits your target market can be tough. If the station has a good market share in your demographic, expect to pay more for the advertising. Trust me on this. Radio stations are not just sitting around waiting to give away advertising to civic organization. They might throw in a few free spots if you make a purchase from them but you cannot expect a free ride. If I have heard it once, I've heard it a thousand times. Someone in your organization who has no clue at all will say something like: "they ought to be glad to advertise our event for free because it's for a good cause." Think about how many civic groups put on local events in your area. If they give free advertising to one, they must give it to all of them. They are primarily in business to make money, not support the community. Since many radio stations are part of a regional or national chain of stations, there is even less chance that they will give you a significant amount of free advertising.

Don't let your personal taste in music interfere with making a logical advertising decision. I don't listen to country music yet I spend my advertising budget there if it hits my target demographic. County fairs, rodeos, horse shows, and blue grass or country concerts all should be advertised on country stations. In the Memphis area, there is a large population of Hispanics. Hispanics generally love to attend county fairs, rodeos, and horse shows. There was only one Hispanic language radio station in the area so reaching that demographic was pretty simple. On the other hand, country stations, rock stations, oldies stations, classic rock stations etc. seem to be a dime a dozen. They split up their target demographic so much that it's hard to reach a significant number of them if you spend your money on only one station. Don't forget to ask your radio station for some trade-outs. Provide them with free passes or t-shirts to give away live on the air. This will make it more likely that people will hear of your event and it stretches your advertising budget.

The days of using posters and newspaper ads for promoting your event are just about dead. If you make a poster large enough to catch someone's eye, then it is very hard to get a store to allow you to hang it up where their customers will see it. You can't put them on telephone poles in most areas because it's against the law. Newspaper advertising is very expensive and many people simply do not read the printed newspaper anymore. If you do use the newspaper for advertising, see if they have an events section. Many papers have a weekly insert that is filled with advertising about local events. Some people will actually purchase the paper just to get access to the weekly insert just like some people only buy the paper on coupon day. If you can't afford a big advertisement in the paper, then you are just wasting your money. Small ads are just lost in the background clutter. If you are lucky, you may be able to get the paper to actually run a story about your event. Even though they say there is no connection between advertising sales and the news, most of the time they won't run a "story" about your event if you haven't made an advertising purchase.

I would like to be able to say that advertising your event will be easy. It won't be. A few years ago, I spent over $30,000 advertising a new, four day fair in the Memphis area. We used advertising banners, fair posters, two high traffic billboards, television commercials, radio spots, newspaper ads in nine different papers, and even letters sent to area churches inviting the faithful to this clean, family oriented event. After all, they were always complaining that there were no family events in the area. The fair was sponsored by the American Legion and was put on in a highly visible area. Because I had one chance to make a good first impression, I put together an awesome lineup of over thirty five major rides, more than forty concessions and games, local vendors and displays, several free live music acts and a free petting zoo. I even had free parking. What I didn't take into consideration was that a little flea bag carnival had played in that town, once a year, for about the last ten years. They had about eight rides total, a few games and concessions and nothing else. Local people just assumed that my fair was that little flea bag show. They turned off their brain immediately upon hearing the words carnival rides. In spite of that, we still made money, put on a great event, and had about 5,500 people at $7 per head, pay to attend. That is not to say that I was satisfied with the results because it should have done much more. I really expected 15,000 people or more at the first event.

The comment that ate at me the most was one that I heard many times during those four days. **"This is a really nice fair! It's a shame you didn't advertise.."**

11. **Establish a timetable for your event**. First you set a date for your event. Next you decide on the date you want to begin advertising your event. Figure out how early you want to begin selling advance tickets. Plan how often you will meet with

your committee to discuss progress and any problems that might develop. Establish dates for training the people who will actually work the event. Let people know when they will be required and for how long. Remember to establish a period for clean-up after your event. You don't want to have to clean up all by yourself!

Your advertising campaign should begin with a few "teasers" about a month before the event and build to a deluge of advertising the week of the event. If you use billboards, you should have them up not more than a month before the event. It takes people a while to notice billboards, but they blend into the scenery pretty fast. The fancy new electronic ones seem to gather the most attention but your advertisement will be one of many that rotate during the day. They still seem to work better than most traditional billboards. As with anything, location is key to the success or failure of billboards. If your billboard is in a crowded area, it will blend into the background and not be noticed even though it is in plain sight. A great location for a billboard is across from a stop sign or traffic signal. If cars have to sit still for awhile, the occupants are more likely to actually read the message on your billboard. Never put too much information on a billboard. The more they say, the less information will be retained as you drive by in your car, listening to the radio, and thinking about your day at the office.

Any newspaper advertising or stories that you were lucky enough to plant with the paper should begin the weekend before your event. If you place it too early, people will forget about your event by the time it actually occurs. When you develop a timeline up front, it makes it easy to make sure that you do everything you need to do on time and on target. The first year of an event is obviously the hardest but keeping good records will make each year's event easier and easier to put on.

12. **Maintain high morale within your organization**. Lunch meetings are great for brainstorming and generally keeping spirits high as your project unfolds. If your committee members lose the feeling that their jobs are important or that the parent organization doesn't really care about the success or failure of your project, then they will not work up to their full potential. Keep them pumped up and see the positive results of your efforts. I usually have custom t-shirts printed and I give them to my event workers. They only cost around $5 when purchased in bulk quantities but I have seen some of my volunteers wear those shirts proudly for years. Another benefit is that the t-shirts also remind people about your event.

Never plan your events too close together. Every organization that I've dealt with has a limited number of really active members who try to do everything. If you have multiple events that are too close together, you will split up your available workforce as each member has to decide which event is more important to them personally. Unfortunately, many people have no business sense whatsoever. They will think that one project is just as important as another. Don't allow this problem to develop. If you are trying to make a big chunk of your organization's annual budget on one event, then you had better maintain focus on that event. Wise leadership must prevail.

13. **Appoint a project manager with decision making authority to actually run the event**. Did you ever hear the story of the committee that tried to build a better horse? When the committee members got through putting in their ideas on improvements that would make the horse a better creature, they created the camel. If you have ever been around a camel then you know it is certainly not an improved version of the horse.

During any event there must be one person in charge. A well planned event will almost run itself but someone has to have the authority to make last minute decisions. It is nearly impossible to ask for a consensus from all the committee members before decisions can be made. There is usually no time for that. Obviously this person must have the full confidence of the committee. While a committee can effectively plan and develop an event, it is the least effective method of actually executing an event. The project manager is the single most important individual during execution of your event. Be sure that you choose a good one. This person does not have to be the most popular person in your club. The project manager should be a person who is very knowledgeable about your event and is level headed enough to be able to consider the facts and make rational decisions quickly. Remember that a fund raising event is business and must be operated as a business. That is the only way it can be successful.

14. **Present the event**. The time has finally arrived to see your careful planning pay off. How well you planned and how well you executed those plans will have a mighty impact on the success or failure of your event. No matter how good your plan is, expect the possibility that some last minute changes must be made. It's the nature of the business. There will always be someone who doesn't show up on time (or at all). Local officials may suddenly say that your parking plan must be changed. You may learn that the food venders that you contracted with don't meet health code requirements. I have had experiences where one set of health code inspectors

approved a food operation and then a different person from the same office comes by and closes them down. These things have always happened and will always happen. You have to take them in stride and then make notes so you can avoid the situation next time.

15. **Keep good records**. Be sure to write down all your contact names, phone numbers and email addresses. Make notes about how to best contact them. Some people only respond to text messages these days while others use email. This is an important detail to remember if you don't want to get frustrated when trying to plan next year's event. If you write down a radio station, newspaper, or billboard company, be sure to include the actual contact person at that organization. Since your contacts are actually sales people, they rarely share their client information with the other staff members there. Include in your notes how much each service cost you. What did you get for the money? Did they include any trade-offs? Did you get any contributions, major discounts, or free mentions of your event? All this historical knowledge is critical when you are trying to negotiate your next deal.

Each year you should build your information base. That will make each year's event easier to stage and it will help you establish a viable community network that supports your event. One of the local charities I worked with had a great sponsor who gave them about $3,000 per year to support a Christmas Shopping Spree for underprivileged children. They did not receive that support one year simply because they had a large change in membership and no one knew who to contact to solicit the contribution. Another year, that same club forgot to invite the sponsor to attend the event and again, lost their support. Careful record keeping can keep this kind of nonsense at a minimum.

16. **Wrap up the event**. Be sure to show your appreciation for the work put into your fund raising program. Letters of appreciation don't cost much but they pay big dividends in the long run. Don't forget to publicly recognize all the business concerns and influential citizens who help make your programs a success. After I got one organization back on their feet financially, we established an annual banquet where we recognized everyone who worked on any of our projects or supported our projects financially. A steak dinner, live music, and some inexpensive plaques made it much easier to ask those people for support for future events. This little awards banquet also improved the organizations image in the community. They went from appearing to be a bunch of beggars to being viewed as a group that was important to the

community. Keeping good records and providing recognition for hard work and other contributions will be the most important ingredients in making your fund raising programs successful now, and in the future.

The Generic 300 Club

An easy way to net $5,000 or more.

The Generic 300 Club is one of the most productive and low risk fund raising projects discussed in this book. It requires low initial investment, performs multiple services to the community, and is a recurring event which becomes easier to stage as the years go by.

I call this idea the Generic 300 Club because the name changes to fit your organization. For example, the Podunk Athletic Booster Club will call it the Podunk 300 Club. The Jaycees might call it the Jaycee 300 Club. The name is not as important as the concept. It is only a label to describe one of the best fund raising ideas around today. It combines the positive aspect of requiring very little money up front with a program which will appeal to a wide spectrum of contributors.

The greater the number of members actively involved in this fund raising effort, the easier it will be to achieve your goal of raising a lot of money for your club. Organizations with a small, active membership will probably have a difficult time with this project. Although I have seen this plan work with only five members doing all the work, I really don't recommend it. Those five members had to dedicate every waking hour for several weeks to make this project a success. After they did it once, they swore they would never do it again.

The selection of a sales chairman, banquet chairman, and promotions chairman should be accomplished as early in the process as possible. They will need all the time they can get to be able to do a good job at their assigned task. By breaking up the overall project into specialized tasks, you make it much simpler for each chairman to handle.

The sales chairman must plan a campaign which will result in the sale of the planned number of tickets. To better reach your sales goal, the chairman should divide the available sales force into teams. These teams should include some "old hands" as well as some people with limited experience. Give each team a few good leads, such as individual names or business concerns which have supported your organization in the past. It makes it easier to make sales when your sales force has confidence. A few easy sales early in the campaign can make a big difference in your team's attitude and eventual success or failure.

A useful sales technique is to show a business what its competition is doing. In a smaller community, they will not want to be the only business which does not support a worthwhile community project. When I was editor of a small magazine, I would sometimes give free advertising to one business in a mall or shopping plaza. I then gave copies of the magazine to every business in the area. When they saw the first business advertising in my magazine, they asked how much it would cost for them to be in the next edition. Advertising sales rose 800% in just one month and remained high as long as I was there. You can use a similar technique to inspire local business to support your events. Make a brochure that shows them the recognition their business will receive. More importantly, include pictures of the annual banquet where you recognized contributors from the year before. As they say, a picture is worth a thousand words.

The promotions chairman must spread the word about your organization, what it does for the community, and information about your current fund raising program. **Sometimes telling what you are going to do with the money is more important than what the actual project is.** For example, I have known people who will sponsor anything that benefits veterans. They don't really care what you are doing today as long as it eventually benefits veterans. A lot of people feel the same way about schools, local sports teams, underprivileged children and so forth. The greater the visibility of your organization in the local community, the easier time your sales force will have in meeting their sales goals. Enhanced name recognition based on your clubs contributions to your community will add to your ability to improve your fiscal bottom line. By all means you should make money on your fund raising projects but you should always invest the proceeds in your local community.

If at all possible, get a popular local personality to be the spokesperson for your group. Take advantage of any positive means of spreading the word about your group and what it is doing for your community. Don't be afraid to list your other successful community projects as well as future plans. Through the efforts of a good publicity chairman, you increase public awareness of your efforts and increase the chances of receiving community support for your project.

To begin the Generic 300 Club project, you must secure 300 sequentially numbered tickets. Although you could probably sell more than 300 tickets in some areas, just about any community large enough to have civic organizations can support sales in this range. If you are developing a program for a really large school or community and feel that you can sell more than 300 tickets, then by all means expand the number to 400, 500 or even more. The principles for a successful project remain the same.

The members of your organization must approach interested members of your community and sell the 300 memberships in the Generic 300 Club for $50 each. I stress the word <u>interested</u> because it simply makes sense to try to sell membership in the club to interested parties. Interested parties will share a common bond. They may be interested in supporting their football team, school band, or any worthwhile community project.

A quick calculation shows that once you sell 300 memberships in your club you will have $15,000 in the bank. The question is, "What do the members of the Generic 300 Club receive for their $50?" The first thing each member receives is the chance to turn that $50 into $100! Americans are very fond of a chance to turn $50 into $100 so this alone may be enough motivation to help you sell your 300 tickets. Each week for thirty-six weeks total, you have a drawing and award one member of the Generic 300 Club a brand new $100 bill. This accomplishes several purposes. First of all, it keeps your club on the minds of all its members and potential members for an extended period of time. That makes it easier to sell memberships in future years. Next, it offers club members the opportunity to support a noble cause while having the potential to double their initial investment. Finally, the psychological impact of awarding crisp, new $100 bills is not to be overlooked.

In addition to the chance to win one of the thirty-six weekly $100 bills, your organization will also sponsor three $1,000 scholarships to deserving graduates of local high schools. These could include an athletic scholarship, band scholarship, and an actual academic scholarship. These three types of scholarships were recommended because each has a devoted base of community support for the programs they represent. In many communities, the most devoted of these groups is the band boosters. Even if the band boosters are not as active as some other groups, usually the band has more members than the other groups. When selecting the graduates to award scholarships, it is important that you involve the community by asking them for nominations. You could also include members of each booster organization on the selection committee. To gain status for your scholarship effort, make it a rule that your scholarship will go to someone that did not receive other monetary scholarships. Do not allow your scholarship to go to someone who applies for everything and ends up with several awards. You may even decide to award six $500 scholarships so more people receive assistance. The local community will appreciate you spreading the wealth this way.

Once a year, you should put on an event to honor members of the Generic 300 Club. Each member should be allowed one guest at the event. When you send out invitations, you should require that they RSVP so you can get a good head count in advance. That helps you make sure you have enough food on hand and helps you keep costs down. You can't automatically assume that 300 members plus one guest each will show up. Planning to feed 600 people when only 200 to 250 show up can be a costly mistake.

I have seen clubs spend all the money generated by the Generic 300 Club project and not put any in their general operating budget. It may be your goal to have a huge banquet style event and just break even overall. If that is your goal, then that is perfectly all right. A program that gives away $3,600 at $100 per week for thirty-six weeks; $3,000 worth of scholarships; and $8,400 for a huge night of entertainment and food; and that pays for itself, is a great win for your organization and community. On the other hand, you can easily hire a decent local band and put out a great array of finger food and drinks and keep up to $5,000 for your organization. It's really up to you and what your club decides it wants to do.

During the evening's entertainment, you will have other opportunities to make a few bucks. Fifty/fifty drawings are pretty common at these events. Any time you get a large group together, a drawing of this type is popular. Buy a double roll of numbered tickets and sell each ticket for $1. The more tickets you sell, the bigger the prize is and the more money the club makes. At one event I attended, the fifty/fifty drawing earned the club a couple of hundred dollars and made one attendee very happy! You can also sell chances to win a vacation, shotgun, or other prizes to be given away during the night. This satisfies a craving to gamble that a lot of people seem to have. They also know that they are contributing to a good cause even if they don't win. Try your best to get your raffle items donated or at least purchase them at a deep discount. Don't make the mistake of buying a high dollar item that requires too many $1 sales just to cover the purchase price. While it should be fun for everyone, you must remember to leave your organization a good chance at making a profit. Don't forget to award the scholarships at this event so that you get more community visibility for your efforts.

If you follow these steps, your organization can earn a profit of around $5,000. Look at the financial breakdown below.

    Income - 300 memberships at $50 each equals $15,000.

    Expense - Tickets, food, and entertainment $3,400 (or more if breaking even is your overall goal); plus thirty-six drawings for $100 each $3,600. Remember that you can draw for less than 36 weeks and increase your profit. It's up to you.

Scholarships - $3,000 worth of scholarships. Three scholarships for $1,000 each or six scholarships for $500. You decide to this or even award more!

NET PROFIT: $5,000 if you follow my recommendations but no less than break even for a year's worth of great community involvement!

As you can see, this fund raising idea can be tailored to your situation. You can easily expand the number of memberships from 300 to 400 to 500 or even more! You just can't change the number once you start. People want to know what their odds are up front so you can't change the parameters once the sale begins. If your only purpose is funding scholarships, you can increase the number granted or the dollar amount of each one. It's all up to you! If you don't think that your community will be excited about supporting scholarships, then reduce or eliminate them from your plan.

If you want a big banquet type event and don't want to save money on the food, you can always have it catered. It will cost at least double but that doesn't matter if that is what you planned. This plan is really easy to adjust to meet your local needs and has proven to be effective. The Generic 300 Club idea is flexible, has a low up-front cost (which translates to low risk), and can provide a relatively large net profit for your organization to use on other community projects. Once your community sees the results of successful execution of the Generic 300 Club, you will see your fund raising problems evaporate. People will ask you if it is time yet to sign up for next year's membership.

If you want to make membership in your Generic 300 Club seem a little more special, consider having a handsome membership certificate printed. If you do have something printed, remember that you want it to look expensive. That doesn't mean it has to be expensive. It just can't look like something you ran off on the office copier at work. You want the Generic 300 Club members to proudly display their membership certificate year round! It should be nice enough that it makes people ask how they can get one. You could give them official ball caps or stadium cushions with your Club's name on them. It's up to you to decide what will appeal to your potential customers.

If you only use one fund raising idea from this book, the Generic 300 Club should be the one. If it was the only project outlined, the purchase of this book would be money well spent. Don't go away quite yet! There are many more proven fund raising ideas in the sections to come.

SAMPLE LETTER

Date:

Dear Southside Panthers Fan:

Please take this opportunity to join us in building a scholarship fund for Southside High School Students. Your membership in the Southside 300 Club will help three deserving graduating seniors get a head start on a college education or training in a vocational field.

Three students will each receive a $1,000 scholarship to be used at the school of their choice. One scholarship recipient will be selected from the varsity athletic program; one from the music program; and one based totally on academics. The scholarship winners will be announced at the annual awards ceremony in May.

In addition to taking pride in knowing that you are helping three deserving students achieve their educational goals, you will also receive:

A membership card identifying you as a Southside 300 Club member.

A Southside 300 Club cap that you can wear while showing everyone your support for the advancement of our students' education.

A stadium cushion to aid in your comfort while attending school functions.

An invitation to attend the annual social event where the scholarships will be awarded.

The opportunity to participate in the 36 weekly drawings for $100. One drawing will be held each Friday during the school year and a lucky Southside 300 Club member will win $100!

Your annual membership fee of $50 will benefit not only the scholarship winners but every student at Southside High School. Funds generated by the Southside 300 Club will be also used to finance special projects and to pay for miscellaneous school expenses. All expenditures will be approved by the booster club executive committee. Please complete the membership application provided below and mail it in or turn it in to the school. Your support is urgently needed and will be of tremendous benefit to many of our great young people. Thanks for your consideration.

Principal	Booster Club President
Southside High School	Southside 300 Club

Southside 300 Club Membership Application

NAME_____

ADDRESS_____PHONE_____

ORGANIZATION EVENT P&L SHEET

Organization_____

Event_____

Date_____Location_____

RECEIPTS:

    Total Number of Tickets Sold @ $_____ Gross Sales_____

    Total Number of Tickets Sold @ $_____ Gross Sales_____

    Total Number of Tickets Sold @ $_____ Gross Sales_____

                    TOTAL TICKET GROSS SALES_____

    Other Cash Receipts   _____

    Other Cash Receipts   _____

    Other Cash Receipts   _____

                    TOTAL CASH RECEIPTS FOR EVENT_____

EXPENSES:

Rent_____
Labor_____
Printing_____
Advertising_____
License_____
_____
_____
_____
_____

                                 TOTAL EXPENSES_____

Total Receipts minus Expenses =   NET PROFIT_____

PROJECT EVALUATION

PROJECT TITLE _____

DATE HELD_____LOCATION_____

TOTAL REVENUE $_____

TOTAL EXPENSES $_____

NET PROFIT $_____

Problems that should corrected:
_____
_____
_____
_____
_____
_____
_____
_____
_____

Project Summary:
_____
_____
_____
_____
_____
_____
_____
_____
_____

Project Chairperson_____

Signature_____

Date_____

RUMMAGE SALES

Transform this neighborhood staple into a major fund raising event!

The main strength of rummage sales is that most of the items sold are donated. This project lends itself to becoming an annual event sponsored by local business and individual contributors. Your profits are limited only by the quality and quantity of the items for sale.

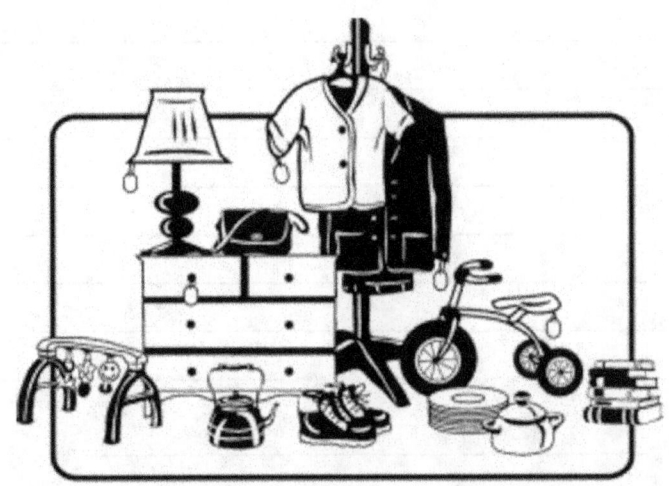

Rummage Sale

Rummage sales have become a very common sight during the past several years. At first, someone decided to try to sell the junk they removed from various storage areas around the home. The idea caught on and people began to band together to sell their items. Thus the flea market was born. In various parts of the country, the flea market has fallen on hard times, but the charity rummage sale is still going strong.

The main strength of the rummage sale is that most of the items sold are donated. Your only cost is picking up the donated items and advertising the event. This is a pretty straight forward idea, but there are some tricks to make it more lucrative for your organization. Here are some suggestions that can transform a simple rummage sale into a major fund raising event.

Make sure that the items for sale are not junk. Get an early start on collecting the items to be included in your rummage sale. You need to have plenty of time for clean-up of the items you choose to sell and time for removal of items not up to your standards. To determine which items are good enough to sell, ask yourself the question, "Would I pay money for this item?" If you would not pay money for an item, how can you expect others to do so? You should approach affluent members of your community with the idea of contributing some items of significant value to be auctioned off at the rummage sale. It is not unheard of for wealthy members of the business community to donate an all expense paid cruise or resort vacation. Someone might donate a moderately expensive piece of jewelry or furniture for your sale. You must convince them that they will be doing a good thing for the community and that they can receive a tax write-off while doing so. All successful business organizations engage in promotional projects. It is up to you to convince them that your project is the one they should sponsor. They will want their involvement in community support projects to be well publicized. Be sure everyone knows how important that business is to the well being of the local community. Let the public know that the business owner wants to give back to the community that makes the success of their business possible.

There are two basic types of sponsorship. Direct sponsorship refers to sponsors who will underwrite all or a major share of the cost of putting on your event, in return for being named as primary sponsors. They actually give you money to support your project. Indirect sponsorship refers to a limited amount of support such as providing some advertising space, use of equipment at a discount or for free, or discounted or free use of a facility and so on.

Some of the benefits which sponsor may receive include:

1. Tax write-offs.
2. Free or reduced rate tickets to be used in their in-store promotions.
3. Favorable public relations.
4. Community recognition.
5. Affiliation with your local civic organization.
6. Positive media exposure at little or no cost.
7. Inclusion of the contributor's logo on advertising material for your event.
8. Recognition at the event. Including on site banners, PA announcements etc.

In-depth knowledge of the benefits available to your potential sponsors will make it much easier for you to get the financial support from the community that you need to be able to put on a successful event. Most people enjoy supporting a good cause. They will enjoy it a lot more when their business stands to benefit from that support!

Your rummage sale must be perceived to be a cut above the average yard sale. That is key to your organization making maximum profit from this event. Having an abundant supply of high quality items to sell is only the beginning. You must also have a great location for your sale. Remember, a major key to business success is location, location, location! This is just as true for your fund raising effort as it is for locating the site of a new Walmart. Unless you have a celebrity in your community who will let you hold your sale in their front yard, then you need to find a better location that is available that day. If you can arrange it, have your rummage sale at the country club, in front of a mega-church, or at a local community center. It must be held in a place which seems special to the attendees for best results. People will pay more money for items they buy at the country club than they will in someone's front yard. It's just human nature. Make it special and it's worth more money. To set the proper tone for your event, be sure to personally contact affluent members of your community and invite them to your event. Let them know what kind of high quality items will be available. A Facebook page or website for your event will also reap dividends. Personal invitations will make attendance more likely by the citizens that you need to attend your event. Obviously, this advice is good for any fund raising event you put on and not just for rummage sales.

To set the tone for a really upscale rummage sale, you might have wine and hors d'oeuvres available and suitable music playing softly in the background. If you are having your sale at a mega-church you should leave out the wine and substitute some other suitable beverage. Conduct the sale at a leisurely pace. This is most important, because the people you want to attract do not wish to be rushed.

Atmosphere, location, perceptions of the clientele, and quality/type of items offered will determine the eventual success or failure of your rummage sale. By following the steps outlined in the past few pages, you can transform your simple yard sale into a successful financial and social event. The sale could turn into an eagerly anticipated annual event, looked forward to by the whole community!

I will not attempt an economic projection based on the successful implementation of a rummage sale. There are just too many variables that effect your financial outcome. You might declare success if you raise $200 or $2,000. The target profit is for your club to decide based on your needs and the items you have to sell. There really is no limit to how much you can generate with a rummage sale. It just depends on quality, quantity, location, advertising, and good weather. Most of these you can control. Remember to start early and work hard to get support from local business. Don't ignore the recommendations outlined here and you have a good chance of having a successful event.

ORGANIZATION EVENT P&L SHEET

Organization_____

Event_____

Date_____Location_____

RECEIPTS:

    Total Number of Tickets Sold @ $_____ Gross Sales_____

    Total Number of Tickets Sold @ $_____ Gross Sales_____

    Total Number of Tickets Sold @ $_____ Gross Sales_____

                       TOTAL TICKET GROSS SALES_____

    Other Cash Receipts   _____

    Other Cash Receipts   _____

    Other Cash Receipts   _____

                TOTAL CASH RECEIPTS FOR EVENT_____

EXPENSES:
Rent_____
Labor_____
Printing_____
Advertising_____
License_____
_____
_____
_____
_____
_____

                                    TOTAL EXPENSES_____

Total Receipts minus Expenses =   NET PROFIT_____

PROJECT EVALUATION

PROJECT TITLE _____

DATE HELD_____ LOCATION_____

TOTAL REVENUE $_____

TOTAL EXPENSES $_____

NET PROFIT $_____

Problems that should corrected:

_____
_____
_____
_____
_____
_____
_____
_____
_____

Project Summary:

_____
_____
_____
_____
_____
_____
_____
_____

Project Chairperson_____

Signature_____

Date_____

Direct Mail Campaigns

Build a solid base of contributors who donate to your organization year after year.

Use your organization's records to keep track of past contributors to your club's projects and events. That information will improve your odds of success tremendously! Target individuals and organizations who have made contributions in the past and you could easily double or triple your positive response rate. Don't overdo it! This type of fund raiser should only be used once per year and no more.

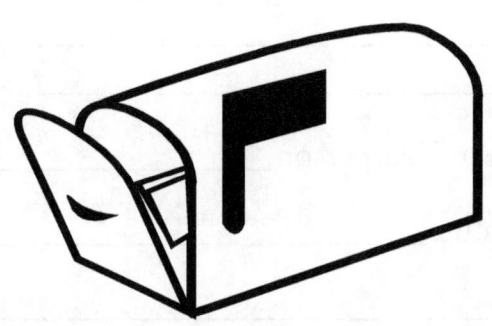

Sometimes we overlook an idea as simple and straight forward as the direct mail campaign. There are many professional fund raising organizations that will be glad to plan and execute such a campaign for your civic club. The drawback to that is the fund raising organization usually keeps most of the money raised and your club gets a small percentage of gross receipts. It is not unusual for expenses with a professional fund raising organization to run as high as 90%.

One of the most common types of direct mail campaigns involves sending something "free" to a list of potential contributors and then asking for a "donation." I have seen organizations send out mail labels, calendars, or holiday cards to their carefully compiled list, accompanied by a plea for contributions. They usually include a list of suggested levels of giving. The idea is to make it simple for the potential contributor. Just pick a level and write a check. Most list at least three levels of giving. Even the lowest level response covers the cost of the mailing plus some amount of money for your club. As mentioned earlier, there are plenty of organizations that will be glad to do this for your club if you can provide them a good list of potential contributors. For example, The American Legion uses their national membership information as a target list. Any of the larger organizations can do the same thing.

Another example of direct mail fund raising was demonstrated by a volunteer fire department in a rural Tennessee community. They get a list of everyone who lives in their fire district and send out an annual letter requesting contributions. They suggest that an appropriate donation would be $50 per household. In the letter they describe what the money is to be used for and the possibility that they won't be able to respond to fires if they do not receive the requested donation. When the consequences are outlined in stark terms such as these, people usually respond with a donation.

The keys to success in a direct mail campaign are relatively simple. Tell the people what you want them to do. If you want them to give money then you should say how much money you are seeking. Tell them what you will use the donations for. Describe what will happen or won't happen if you don't reach the amount of money you are attempting to raise. Make it easy for people to give. Tell them exactly how, when, and where contributions can be made. Give people choices of different levels of giving. If given three choices, most people will select the middle one. Plan accordingly. Make sure that you let people know there is a deadline for responding to your solicitation.

One year a Jaycee organization was planning to put on a Christmas Shopping Spree for underprivileged children. When they sent out their direct mail solicitations, they forgot to tell people when the event would be held. Without a specific date to respond on the solicitation, people just kept putting off their donations until the proposed event had come and gone. The Jaycees were only able to support a fraction of the children that they normally provided a happy Christmas for. Think about what that simple omission cost. Read and re-read your direct mail solicitation and remove anything that can cause it to fail or make it hard to respond to. As we say in sales, "remove the objections." Don't give people an excuse to ignore your request for support.

Another key ingredient to a great direct mail letter is to highlight what your organization has done for your community in the past. It follows that you will also want to describe what you plan to do in the future as well.

As always, keep good records of who gives and who doesn't. Good records will make it easier for the next chairman to also have a successful fund raising event. Many times I have seen a good chairman execute a great fund raising project, and then fail to pass on the keys to success to subsequent chairmen. Many times it is a simple oversight but I have actually seen people who keep important information to themselves because they don't want the next chairman to succeed. Unfortunately, this happens more often than you might think.

In general, I don't really like Direct Mail campaigns. The projects I really like are the ones where you provide something valuable and EARN money to support your club at the same time. That's why the next project I talk about is the Fair or Carnival.

Sample Direct Mail Letter

Podunk Volunteer Fire Department

Route 3, Podunk, Arkansas

Dear _____: 1 April 2016

Each year the Podunk Volunteer Fire Department provides protection from fires that might destroy your home and everything in it. We are not funded by any government body since we serve people who live in an unincorporated area. Every member of this fire department works without pay to insure your safety. Even without the burden of paying salaries, there are other expenses that we must cover. These include purchasing and maintaining fire-fighting equipment, building improvements and upkeep, utilities, training and more. Without your contributions we would have to shut the doors of our volunteer fire department. That would leave you and your family unprotected. Look at the recommended levels of support listed below. The bottom number is the minimum amount that will keep us afloat. Please consider giving a little more so that we can make improvements to better serve this community. Thanks for taking the time to read and respond to this urgent request for your help.

Contribution Levels

$50 per year _____

$75 per year_____

$100 per year_____

Please enclose your check and mail it in by 1 May 2016 so that we will be able to prepare a budget for the upcoming year. Again, thank you for your support. We can't do it without you.

Bubba Jones

Volunteer Fire Chief

Podunk Volunteer Fire Department

PROJECT EVALUATION

PROJECT TITLE _____

DATE HELD_____LOCATION_____

TOTAL REVENUE $_____

TOTAL EXPENSES $_____

NET PROFIT $_____

Problems that should corrected:

_____
_____
_____
_____
_____
_____
_____
_____

Project Summary:

_____
_____
_____
_____
_____
_____
_____
_____

Project Chairperson_____

Signature_____

Date_____

Fairs and Carnivals

Host a memorable event designed to reach everyone in your local community and earn thousands of dollars for your organization at the same time!

Carnivals and Fairs involve a lot of work but give you an excellent opportunity to serve the community on more than one level. Not only can you make money to support other programs, the Fair or Carnival itself can become an eagerly anticipated annual event.

Many people think of Fairs and Carnivals as "kid stuff." This couldn't be further from the truth. A properly operated Fair or Carnival can be a fund raising gold mine! Don't make the mistake of expecting overnight success or success without a lot of good planning. A well designed and executed Fair or Carnival has unlimited potential as a fund raising tool.

First you need to understand the difference between a Fair and a Carnival. In its most basic form, a Fair is held inside a fenced area and an admission fee is charged for entrance. Once inside, there should be some free attractions like local displays, local venders, live music, a free petting zoo or even free circus acts. Customers may purchase food from approved concessionaires and pay to play individual carnival games. Rides are generally not covered by the gate admission. I say generally because sometimes you may operate a Pay-One-Price admission that covers both gate admission and all rides. Your organization should get a percentage or set amount for everything at the Fair that charges a fee. You can even charge for parking if you choose to.

A carnival is simply a group of rides and concessions sitting in a large open space that you hope people will go to and spend money. You should receive a percentage of the ride gross and some amount for each concession. You will not receive anything for admission but you will not have the expense of providing free entertainment on the grounds. You can charge for parking if you choose to.

With well over twenty years of operating both Fairs and Carnivals I can say unequivocally that establishing and operating a genuine Fair offers the greatest opportunity for making money. That being the case, I will talk about how to run a successful Fair first.

Do your research. Before you try to establish a Fair, first try to find out why there isn't one already. Sounds simple but it's one of the most over looked steps. When I established a County Fair in Anniston, AL in the 1980's, I found that there had actually been a Fair in place for more than fifty years. It was the victim of urban growth. The club that originally operated the Fair made no attempt in fifty years to secure a permanent location. As the city grew, the prime location that they used for many of those years was developed by the property owners for other purposes. The club's lack of foresight in purchasing a permanent location resulted in the Fair moving several times during its last few years of existence. Each time it moved, it got smaller and smaller until it finally became a losing proposition. It was out of business for several years when I got the idea to start it up again. Over the years I have found that scenario played out in many towns and even larger cities like Memphis and Birmingham. The Fair in Memphis was once one of the largest Fairs in America. It ran for over one hundred years close to downtown Memphis. As the city grew up around it and the area around the Fairgrounds became crime ridden, attendance got smaller and smaller. The same thing happened in Birmingham.

To achieve success, location is everything. It must be safe, convenient, and well known. Any of these three factors can make or break you.

Contract with a reputable carnival. There are lots of carnivals out there. Many of them are operated by honorable people while some are definitely not! The carnival is the entity that will provide the rides for your event. It will also bring along some professionally operated carnival games and food concessions. The safest way to know the difference is to ask for references AND then check them. Use the internet to research the carnival and see if they have had problems in other locations. Ask other Fair managers if they know anything about the carnival you are thinking about doing business with.

An American Legion Post that I know tried to put on a Fair this year. They lined up a free petting zoo, local exhibitors, free entertainment and got a good crew together to park cars. The problem was that the carnival didn't show up. The Legion broke a cardinal rule of Fair operations. They did not get a contract from the carnival months in advance of the date. When the carnival kept promising a contract and didn't deliver one, the American Legion Post should have suspected that something wasn't right. What they later found out was the carnival that they featured in their advertising, set up in a shopping center a few miles away and ran without having to pay a sponsor anything. They got the benefit of American Legion advertising and word of mouth but didn't pay the Legion anything. Don't get caught in that trap. Get a contract with a reputable carnival for specific dates before you take another step.

You must watch every expense and get as much free stuff as you possibly can. Often overlooked is the cost of renting a stage for your free acts to perform on. Stage rental can easily run more than $1000 for your event. Why pay for a stage when you may be able to get one for free. If the local recreation department is a co-sponsor of your Fair then they may let you use their stage. It may only be an old flatbed trailer but in most cases, that is all you need. Unless you are using high dollar, professional entertainment there is no point in spending thousands of dollars to rent a state of the art stage.

Media sponsors save you money. Try to get a local TV or radio station to be a sponsor of your event. They will often offer discounted advertising if they understand what your organization is planning to do with the proceeds. Notice I said "discounted." The days of "FREE" advertising are long over for the most part. Many times I hear people in civic organizations wisely expound, "They ought to advertise that for free since it's for a good cause!" Every local group and civic organization thinks that. If the local radio or TV station gives their advertising free to one group then all groups expect the same treatment. They simply can't afford to give their advertising away. That doesn't mean that you can't work out a sponsorship arrangement where it looks like the radio or TV station is deeply involved when all you are getting from them is a discount on advertising you pay for. It makes the radio and TV station look good and even adds a level of prestige and respectability to your event when the customers think it is partially sponsored by these entities.

It's important to note that though the advertising department and the news department of these organizations are supposed to be totally separate, you will find it is easier to get "news" coverage if you are buying advertising from them. This applies to radio, TV, and even the venerable newspaper.

Create levels of sponsorship. Keep in mind that people prefer to give in round numbers. It may help sponsorships if you establish a graduated system. You may name them something like "Bronze Sponsor" at the lowest level; "Silver Sponsor" at the next level; "Gold Sponsor" and finally, "Platinum Sponsor" at the highest level. What you call them is not really important. Listing sponsors by the level of their support encourages some to give more just for the bragging rights. I normally have banners printed with the names of all sponsors listed by the level of their sponsorship. These banners are proudly displayed near the entrance to the Fair so that everyone who attends will see them. Be sure to create appropriate awards for each level of giving. The bigger the amount, the greater the recognition. Don't try to be cheap. Appropriate recognition will help you today and in the future.

If you are really lucky and have excellent connections with a large business entity such as an automobile dealership or local factory, you may even be able to secure a sponsorship worth thousands of dollars. You can do this by recognizing the major sponsor as presenting all the free entertainment. You may say that a discounted gate admission was complements of a certain sponsor. You may have a "Free Ride Night" that is sponsored by a specific entity.

FREE RIDE NIGHT! The Free Ride Night concept is the single greatest promotional tool I have ever came up with. The County Fair that I operated was a ten day event for many years. That way I could have two weekends. Business during weeknights was very slow since it was in a small community where people didn't have a lot of extra money for entertainment. On a typical Thursday night approximately one hundred people would pay the admission and come to the Fair. This was the norm for about ten years. Normally I would keep all the gate admission and get about 25% of the ride gross from the carnival. The idea of having a Pay-One-Price that covered gate admission and all the rides was not a new one. Calling it "FREE RIDE NIGHT" and saying it was sponsored by a specific entity was what made it special. People love to think they are getting something for free. Anyone in advertising will tell you that FREE is the most powerful word in advertising. The first time I offered FREE RIDE NIGHT, attendance went from one hundred on Thursday night to six hundred and fifty! For the next three years I kept the price the same and the results were the same. Approximately six hundred and fifty patrons on Thursday night. That's when I had my next idea. It concerns "perception of value." Originally, I made a mistake by pricing the FREE RIDE NIGHT admission too low! When I doubled the price, the number of patrons actually increased to over sixteen hundred on FREE RIDE NIGHT. When it cost more, people thought it was worth more. Attendance on FREE RIDE NIGHT stayed at that level until I moved to another state and closed the Fair. Even though I split the "FREE RIDE" money 50/50 with the carnival, we both made a lot more money on this normally slow day. Never be afraid to think out of the box.

Potential revenue from Fairs A successful fair has many potential revenue streams. Make sure you tap into as many of them as you can without appearing greedy. Your organization should get a percentage of the ride gross from the carnival. The carnival charges each of the food concessionaires and game operators for the privilege of operating during the fair. You should get some of that money since you will normally incur the expense of water and electricity to support those games and food concessions. You should keep all revenue from gate admission. Remember to keep your gate admission reasonable. You can also charge for parking and keep the money. However, I never charge for parking if I am charging a gate admission. You don't want to seem to be greedy, charging for everything in sight! You should keep revenue derived from renting space for local exhibits and local food operations. Most carnivals will not want you to book local food operations since they would detract from theirs. If they agree to allow you to book local food joints then they must charge the same price for similar items as the professional carnival food concessions. For example if the carnival charges two dollars for a soft drink then your local food booths must charge two dollars. Although it takes away competition and ends up costing the customer more money, you must do this to keep the carnival happy.

The carnival world is very competitive these days. Many of the smaller shows have folded due to higher cost of operations. That means there are not enough carnivals around to play the dates available. They are constantly looking to improve their route with dates that gross more money. In past years it was not uncommon for a carnival to play the same date, for the same club, year after year. With operating costs at an all time high, they can't do that anymore. That's why you must remember that your contract desires must be flexible. Until you have a proven track record you must take a smaller percentage of the ride gross and expect smaller payments for games and concessions.

As a general rule of thumb, I try to cover all the costs incurred in presenting a top quality Fair with money from gate admissions. That leaves the carnival percentages as the profit from the venture. If you receive any local sponsorship, that can be applied to expenses as well.

Plan for all the expenses. This is very hard the first year but should be very easy every year after that. KEEP GOOD RECORDS! I will try to list things you will probably have to pay for.

> Grounds rental. Without a place to put the Fair, you are dead in the water!
>
> Advertising. Do not expect free advertising to be enough. To succeed, you must have paid advertising. After you have established a successful Fair, the carnival will usually chip in some money to help cover advertising cost. You may be on your own the first year.
>
> Entertainment. Even local acts deserve to be paid something. Some performers will perform for exposure but not year after year. Professional

entertainment must be paid for. Don't forget that a stage will cost you money as well. You should establish a daily budget for entertainment and stick to it. Spend the most money on days when you expect attendance to be the greatest.

Electricity and water. Most carnival contracts will require you to provide electricity and water. Plan to pay for it.

License and local taxes. With every government from local to national trying to raise money without raising taxes, expect to pay for a business license and sales tax. Each city is different. Some will waive these fees and some won't. One ten day Fair that I ran cost nearly four thousand dollars for the license alone. In another city the license fee for ten days was totally waived. If your local government is a co-sponsor of the event, your chances of saving a lot of money on license and sales tax is greatly improved. Always point out the benefits of bringing quality, family entertainment to your town or city. It never hurts to ask local government to be a co-sponsor.

Labor. Even though most civic groups operate with volunteers, I have found that it's better to pay security personnel and anybody that handles ticket sales. During one of my first Fairs, local Jaycees were charging for parking. Almost every other dollar went in the pockets of the guys running the parking lot. Since they weren't being paid, they felt justified in taking a little something for themselves. Stealing is stealing. Don't tempt people by placing too much trust in them. You can watch paid employees in a ticket booth but you can't oversee everyone in a parking lot if you are trying to get people parked and into the Fair as quickly as possible. That is yet another reason not to charge for parking.

Insurance. Today's carnivals expect to provide a two million dollar liability policy to cover each event. Make sure that they include your organization and the property owners in the list of insured.

Reach out to other local groups to boost attendance. An easy way to increase attendance at your Fair is to invite other organizations to participate. For example, invite the local high school band to play at the Fair and they will usually bring along several people each. The band gets in free but not the guests. Another way to increase attendance is to offer free booth space to different groups. Again, they will almost always bring along guests. In my first edition of Dynamic Fund Raising Projects (1990), I spent a lot of time telling how to create local game booths. As the years passed, participation in carnival games has really dropped off. At one time, carnival games were really great money makers. Only a relative few have survived the test of time. The best ones are professionally owned and operated. The patter generated by their operators is the main reason for their success. You just can't "build it and they will come" anymore. The only booth that I'd recommend for local civic groups is the rented dunk tank. That will only work if you have an obnoxious person sitting on the bar waiting to be dunked. Either that or a bunch of very attractive scantily clad women. Sometimes a favorite local personality who is willing to get wet for charity can make the dunking booth successful. Only try it if you can get the dunking booth for very low cost. It's just not worth the risk.

Fair layout. The carnival owner is an expert at laying out the rides, games, and concessions so that the whole thing flows. All you have to do is let him know what space you need for your stage and local exhibits. Other than making sure that all campers and bunkhouses are out of sight of the midway, you have very little to worry about in laying out a Fairgrounds.

Carnivals. Carnivals are just simplified versions of the Fair. They are simpler to put on but have fewer opportunities for your organization to make money. There is no gate admission so you miss out on the chance to earn a lot of money. With no gate fee, you just about have to charge for parking. Which would you rather have? Five dollars from every person who enters the Fair or three dollars per carload for parking? For me, it's a no brainer. On the other hand, you don't need to schedule a lot of free entertainment since no one paid anything to be there.

It has always been incredible to me that people still come to a Fair and say, "I'm just going to walk around and look so I shouldn't have to pay anything." Entertainment is what you are selling. Walking around and just looking is entertainment. You deserve to be paid for it. Plus, in a Fair there will be free acts for the patrons to watch. Acts that you had to pay for in one way or another.

Things to remember. Get a signed contract first. Secure a safe and convenient location with plenty of parking. Create an advertising budget. Create an entertainment budget. Figure out how many people you need each day and then find them. Safeguard your cash! Hire security and money handlers. Be sure the carnival gives you a percentage of the ride gross, something for each game and concession, rental for the space used by their campers and bunkhouses, and if possible, ask them to contribute to the advertising budget. It never hurts to ask. All they can say is yes or no. The P&L Sheets and Project Evaluation Sheets shown on the next couple of pages were designed for my Fair.

ORGANIZATION EVENT P&L SHEET

Organization_____

Event_____

Date_____Location_____

RECEIPTS:

    Total Number of Tickets Sold @ $_____ Gross Sales_____

    Total Number of Tickets Sold @ $_____ Gross Sales_____

    Total Number of Tickets Sold @ $_____ Gross Sales_____

                  TOTAL TICKET GROSS SALES_____

    Other Cash Receipts   _____

    Other Cash Receipts   _____

    Other Cash Receipts   _____

                  TOTAL CASH RECEIPTS FOR EVENT_____

EXPENSES:

Rent_____
Labor_____
Printing_____
Advertising_____
License_____
_____
_____
_____
_____
_____
_____

                                  TOTAL EXPENSES_____

Total Receipts minus Expenses =   NET PROFIT_____

PROJECT EVALUATION

PROJECT TITLE _____

DATE HELD _____ LOCATION _____

TOTAL REVENUE $_____

TOTAL EXPENSES $_____

NET PROFIT $_____

Problems that should corrected:

_____
_____
_____
_____
_____
_____
_____
_____
_____

Project Summary:

_____
_____
_____
_____
_____
_____
_____
_____
_____

Project Chairperson _____

Signature _____

Date _____

Haunted Houses

Make this an annual event and earn thousands of dollars in one week.

The club members who put on the haunted house enjoy themselves almost as much as the patrons. A well, truly spooky haunted house will attract quite a bit of repeat business, and the whole community will look forward to this as an annual event.

Haunted Houses continue to be a fun and relatively in-expensive way to raise money for your organization. The main problem is that in some areas, local governments are getting into the act. Some require fire inspections and enforce statutes as if they were permanent structures. Obviously, it can be cost prohibitive to put in a sprinkler system for a project that you may use a few days each year. Before you even consider this project, ask other haunted house operators in your area if they have any trouble with local code enforcement. If the coast is clear, then read on for information about Haunted Houses.

Once again, the most important single factor is location. I have seen some of the best haunted houses lose money because of being in a bad location. Sometimes the problem is parking. Your location may be perceived to be in a bad neighborhood. Your haunted house will be much more effective if located in a highly visible, well-traveled area. The old adage, "out of sight, out of mind" is especially true when talking about haunted houses.

There are as many layouts for haunted houses as individual imaginations. The best advice is to keep it simple. Use the physical layout of the building to your advantage. Some buildings are actually huge, empty shells with four walls and a roof. This allows you to exercise your imagination and lay out the rooms and hallways as you see fit. One organization built a simple maze which connected various rooms containing scary sets. The maze was kept dark, had many twists and turns, and added significantly to the scary atmosphere of the haunted house. Just be sure that you keep safety in mind when building it. Remember that they won't be able to see very well inside the maze so it's up to you to keep them safe. Make sure there are no nails, screws, or anything else that a person might cut themselves on while wandering along in the dark.

The maze is a passive type of attraction which requires little or no manpower to operate. Keep in mind that you should try to keep the number of people required to operate your haunted house attraction to a minimum. After all, they will be volunteers and it may be hard to get enough to operate safely for an extended number of days.

Using an old house with many rooms is generally preferable to using a hollow "shell building." You can keep costs much lower by not having to construct a lot of walls. Just design each room as a separate attraction and have enough volunteers around to direct the patrons from room to room. The main drawback to using an existing house is that you are restricted by the physical layout. It may be possible to split larger rooms to create more different experiences within your haunted house. The looks of an old house can attract adventurous customers but it's what's inside that will bring them back over and over again. Customers who keep bringing their family and friends with them are the most important group you will encounter. Develop this group and your economic success is assured.

Here are some ideas for viable attractions within your haunted house. These are not the only ones which will work but each of these is tried and tested. If you appoint room committees or teams, have them compete among themselves for best room design and execution. If you do, you should wind up with a great haunted house. Give a prize to the team with the best design and execution of their plan. This sounds like a small thing but we all love to compete and we all like to receive awards for our efforts. Harness this creative energy for the good of your organization and your community.

> 1. Mock graveyards -- The mock graveyard is a natural attraction in or outside your haunted house. They are usually just outside the entrance or in the first room once you enter the attraction. It will set the tone and establish that creatures of the night may be on the loose. Have some headstones identifying favorite horror movie characters such as *Friday the 13th's* Jason, Freddie Kruger from *Nightmare on Elm Street*, Dracula, the Wolfman, or any others you can think of. Show an open coffin or two to add to the effect. Put a live person in one of the open caskets to interact with the patrons. This should give the customers a good fright so be sure that particular casket is out of reach of the patrons. Some of them might react physically to being scared.

> 2. Texas chainsaw massacre -- An incredibly ugly mask, old clothes, and a real chainsaw (with the cutting chain removed for safety) combine to give you a very scary room. Hang a few props around the room to make it look like a butcher shop and you have a favorite of many haunted house patrons. Start with a dark room. Once a group of patrons are inside, crank the chainsaw and turn on a spot light to illuminate a corner where the killer is standing. He will rev up the chainsaw a few times while making wild swings at the patrons (being careful to never get close to them). To make this room safer, build a waist high wall or fence that separates the chainsaw killer from the patrons. That way they

never try to occupy the same space at the same time. The waist high barrier or chicken wire wall will keep patrons safe and will help keep tension at a peak. In the darkened room no one will really notice it at all.

3. Character spotlights -- Most any horror film character will scare you when encountered unexpectedly. There was a period of time when vampires were all the rage so they were staples of most haunted attractions. Right now it's zombies that are in style so be sure to have plenty around. They don't cost much and people seem to have a lot of fun playing them. Just have your costumed volunteer suddenly appear out of the dark and you will achieve the desired level of scariness. This can be accomplished by use of a strobe light or just suddenly shine a light on a portion of the dark room so the creature is suddenly illuminated.

4. In the past I wrote about the horror staple "Bowl of Guts," "Coffin Spotlight," and the "Rat Pit" as attractions for your haunted house. These have all been around since the fifties and continue to work today. The Rat Pit is the only one that requires a little more explanation. The gist is that you create a short portion of your maze that requires patrons to get down on their hands and knees to pass through. Put down a plexiglass floor so the patrons can see what's underneath them. Under the plexiglass, you should be able to see skulls, bones, and if possible, live rats. You don't need many and live ones may be purchased at a local pet store. This creates a passive display that will scare people but will not require constant attention by a volunteer.

I recommend that you use a costumed volunteer as a host to guide each group of patrons through your attraction. They can control the pace and help you to re-set between groups of viewers. Nothing is worse than having customers enter your room before the ghouls and goblins are ready for them. One thing that can ruin the experience for your patrons is to allow them to see partially costumed characters before or during the haunted house experience. The anticipation and suspension of disbelief is lost when this happens so be careful. Both Disney World and Disney Land are fanatical about keeping the integrity of their costumed characters intact. They are hugely successful so I say, "If it works for them, it will work for you!"

In the past few years I have noticed that the Haunted Forrest has become a viable Halloween fund raising attraction as well. The same basic rules as any Haunted attraction apply. It is just easier to make a walk in the woods, in the dark appear spooky! I have also seen haunted cornfields put on year after year in some locations. There is a huge one located between Memphis and Millington, Tennessee that has been scaring folks and making a lot of money for years. A local farmer plants a huge field of corn and harvests the corn by hand, leaving the stalks in place. In early October, he mows a maze into the cornfield. He uses costumed volunteers to lurk inside the dark maze, scaring patrons and reaping huge profits! It has been going on at least ten years so I know that it is profitable or he wouldn't still be doing it. As the years go by, favorable word of mouth has made it a featured attraction in that area.

Your profit from this type project is limited only by your location and the number of years it has been in place. I have seen civic groups earn their entire annual budget from one week's worth of presenting a haunted attraction. You should plan to spend more at first on advertising than later years. A good haunted attraction will gain fame and word will spread. Many people will return more than once each year as they show their friends what all the excitement is about. Others will plan group trips to your attraction. They will bring their youth groups, sports teams, scout troops, church groups and so on, as they know you will operate a safe and family friendly event. It also doesn't hurt that they know you intend to use the money earned to make their community a better place. More importantly, they will plan to come back each year to see what improvements you have made since last year. You can't just do exactly the same thing each year and continue to grow.

ORGANIZATION EVENT P&L SHEET

Organization_____

Event_____

Date_____Location_____

RECEIPTS:

Total Number of Tickets Sold @ $_____ Gross Sales_____

Total Number of Tickets Sold @ $_____ Gross Sales_____

Total Number of Tickets Sold @ $_____ Gross Sales_____

TOTAL TICKET GROSS SALES_____

Other Cash Receipts   _____

Other Cash Receipts   _____

Other Cash Receipts   _____

TOTAL CASH RECEIPTS FOR EVENT_____

EXPENSES:

Rent_____
Labor_____
Printing_____
Advertising_____
License_____
_____
_____
_____
_____
_____
_____

TOTAL EXPENSES_____

Total Receipts minus Expenses =   NET PROFIT_____

PROJECT EVALUATION

PROJECT TITLE _____

DATE HELD_____LOCATION_____

TOTAL REVENUE $_____

TOTAL EXPENSES $_____

NET PROFIT $_____

Problems that should corrected:
_____
_____
_____
_____
_____
_____
_____
_____
_____

Project Summary:
_____
_____
_____
_____
_____
_____
_____
_____
_____

Project Chairperson_____

Signature_____

Date_____

Custom T-Shirt Sales

The sky's the limit when selling custom T-shirts. You can make a few hundred or a few thousand dollars depending on your initial investment.

Because of our pride in all things local, custom T-shirt sales may be the easiest project to complete successfully. They do require an upfront investment, but T-shirt sales can be an ongoing project which stops earning money only when you want to stop doing it.

There are as many potential customers for custom T-shirts as there are humans on the planet. I own more than twenty different custom T-shirts which I purchased or received as promotional material. Either way, someone paid for them.

The most obvious idea for a custom T-shirt is one that publicizes your organization. Thousand of T-shirts are sold every day that only have some organization's name on them. Your approach to sales of custom T-shirts will depend on your ultimate goal. Do you want to simply make money or do you want to promote your organization? To promote your organization, a simple one-color print on a promotional grade T-shirt will allow you to get your message to more people for less money. You should still be able to get promotional grade T-shirts for around three to four dollars each. There is a list of sources in the last section of this book to help you with your search for cheap T-shirts.

If you want to concentrate on fund raising, you should consider a multi-color print on a better grade of T-shirt. In days past, you would have to pay around $100 for a nice multi-color, camera ready design. With computers doing most of the layout work, most T-shirt companies will do your design for free if you purchase enough T-shirts. Twenty five years ago, when I wrote the first edition of this book, I could purchase a very good quality T-shirt with a three color design for about $4.00 each. You should still be able to get them for $6.00 or less today. Improvements in the process and increased competition created by internet sales have kept current costs lower than the inflation rate for that period. I recently purchased custom T-shirts for the American Legion Fair for about $4.00 each. They were one color print on a very nice quality T-shirt. Use your computer to find the best deals and you are on the way to achieving your organizations goals with T-shirt sales.

What you print on the shirt has as more to do with whether you are successful selling them than any other single aspect of this project. Witty sayings, cute graphics, or just about anything to do with a local or state sports team or youth program will make your shirts fairly easy to sell. You might simply do a one color print of the phrase "I'm Proud To Be A _____Booster" and achieve significant success. By making it obvious what your T-shirt sales support, it makes it easier to sell them. I usually mark up my T-shirts one hundred percent or more. By pricing them around $10 each, they are affordable and leave you with a fair profit for your organization. If you think $10 is too much, check the prices for T-shirts at concerts, theme parks, and so on. Even printed T-shirts on the internet often retail for $20 or more!

Because there is very little difference in the production cost of a good quality T-shirt and a poor quality, promotional grade T-shirt, I always spend a little extra and buy the good stuff. This gives the customer more for their money, encourages repeat sales, and saves your organization a black eye resulting from selling inferior merchandise. The few cents extra that you will make selling cheap T-shirts is just not worth it.

As a civic organization, there are many ways to sell the T-shirts once you have them in hand. Many business concerns will sell them for you on consignment as a way to help the community. This gives you a broader market for your shirts than if you only sell them through one location. Obviously the internet is another great option for selling your shirts. Most organizations have their own website or Facebook page where they can advertise and sell promotional items like T-shirts. If you combine T-shirt sales with another event, you can usually make even more money by raffling a few of them during the event. Sell chances on a $10 shirt for fifty cents each and see how much you take in. Most anybody will buy a fifty cent chance to win a $10 item. Even if you fall a little short of the $10 mark, you probably only have around $5 in the T-shirt so you still make a profit. A wise man once said, "You will never go broke while making a profit!"

Many of the fund raising ideas listed in this book can be combined to provide an integrated fund raising approach. Any special event represents an opportunity to market a commemorative T-shirt. Don't waste these opportunities. Maximize your organization's opportunities to raise money for projects that will benefit the local community!

ORGANIZATION EVENT P&L SHEET

Organization_____

Event_____

Date_____ Location_____

RECEIPTS:

    Total Number of Tickets Sold @ $_____ Gross Sales_____

    Total Number of Tickets Sold @ $_____ Gross Sales_____

    Total Number of Tickets Sold @ $_____ Gross Sales_____

                       TOTAL TICKET GROSS SALES_____

    Other Cash Receipts   _____

    Other Cash Receipts   _____

    Other Cash Receipts   _____

                TOTAL CASH RECEIPTS FOR EVENT_____

EXPENSES:
Rent_____
Labor_____
Printing_____
Advertising_____
License_____
_____
_____
_____
_____
_____

                                    TOTAL EXPENSES_____

Total Receipts minus Expenses =   NET PROFIT_____

PROJECT EVALUATION

PROJECT TITLE _____

DATE HELD_____ LOCATION_____

TOTAL REVENUE $_____

TOTAL EXPENSES $_____

NET PROFIT $_____

Problems that should corrected:

_____
_____
_____
_____
_____
_____
_____
_____

Project Summary:

_____
_____
_____
_____
_____
_____
_____
_____

Project Chairperson_____

Signature_____

Date_____

Concession Stands

A well organized concession stand is easy to run, and can earn you a lot of money.

Do a good job on this project and you may be invited to operate concession stands for other organizations as well. If you don't have a plan, and stick to it, you can lose money and give your organization a black eye in the community. Do it, but do it right!

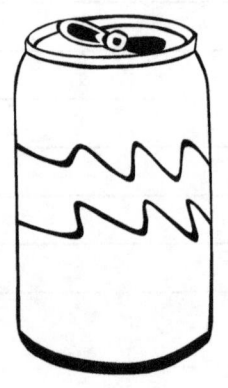 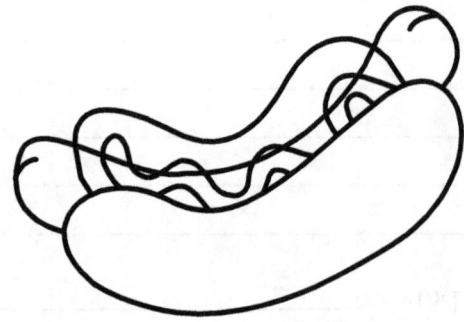

Concession stands are being used all across the nation by every conceivable type of booster club to raise funds. Almost every one of them thinks they are doing a fine job because they take in a lot of money. They do not stop to consider the cost of goods. I have operated concession stands in a wide range of venues for more than twenty-five years. My goal is to keep the overall cost of goods at 25% or less. Strive to reach that goal when planning your product mix.

A local Cub Scout Pack asked me to take a look at the operation of their concession stand. They just could not figure out why they were not making any profit. There was considerable finger pointing going on because no one could figure out why there was no profit although they had a steady stream of customers while they were open. The first place I looked was cost of goods. That is usually the main problem and it was the problem here. Most of the items purchased for resale were purchased in bulk quantities but were never priced out correctly for individual sales. The volunteers operating the concession stand simply charged whatever they wanted to for each item. In this instance, the better business was, the more the Cub Scouts lost.

You must remember that a concession stand is a business and must be operated like a business. Establish the cost of each individual item, then set a selling price that is both reasonable and allows you to make a profit. Keep your price structure as simple as possible. Try to keep your price increments at twenty-five cents. This will allow you to add up the total purchase more easily and you only need to keep quarters on hand to make change. Once you set your prices, post them so everyone can see them. Nothing will frustrate your customers more than paying different prices for the same item, just because a different volunteer waited on you. Posting the prices prominently will help the customer and the server.

When you have volunteers working the concession stand, you can expect that a certain amount of food will be consumed by the volunteers or even given away. This can destroy your profit margin very quickly. At a small convenience store I reviewed, they had a problem with employees eating one or two candy bars from each box of twenty four. To stay competitive, there was very little mark-up on candy. If only two bars were lost from each box of twenty four candy bars, you could sell the other twenty two bars and still not make a profit. Most volunteers won't even think this is stealing, but it is. If you make it plain what the rules are before you begin your operation, you will be much better off in the end. I usually plan for a certain amount of pilferage and figure that into my 25% cost of goods. Humans are humans. Don't be in denial. Just make a plan and you will be all right.

Many organizations rely on donated food items to sell. While it is nice to have donated items, you can still generate a lot of profit from a selection of purchased items.

1. Hot dogs - Even if you purchase your hot dogs and buns off the shelf at the local supermarket, you can have them ready to sell for less than fifty cents, total cost of goods sold. At most special events, football games, races and so on, the simple hotdog sells for up to four dollars each. If you sell yours for two dollars, you earn a very nice profit and still give a good deal to your customers. Don't shortchange your customers by purchasing the cheapest hotdogs you can find. You can still stay under a cost of fifty cents each, even if you use jumbo hotdogs of high quality. You really save very little by purchasing the cheaper hotdogs but you achieve a vast improvement in customer satisfaction by only using high quality products. Make sure that your buns are fresh. Often some well intentioned individual will go to the day old bread store and buy stale buns to save a few bucks. It's just not worth it. You pay a little more for a good quality hotdog and then ruin it by putting it on a dried up bun. Don't do it! My personal favorite hotdog recipe makes use of an old time trick. If you can find a bun steamer, keep your hotdog buns in it. They will be tasty and fresh all day long! The last touch to make your hotdog sales special involves keeping a bountiful supply of condiments on hand so customers can make their hotdogs taste just right. If you have access to the stainless steel pump stations like they use at many fast food restaurants, you should use them. If not, use bottles with squirt heads on them. Individual packages of catsup and mustard are messy and time consuming to use. Most customers prefer to squirt it on. A lot of customers will buy one hotdog to try them out. If it is good, they are likely to purchase one or two more. If the first one is mediocre, they will move on and find something else to spend their money on.

2. Popcorn - A commercial popcorn popper is a good investment for a club if they plan to sell popcorn at events for years to come. The visual of popcorn popping in the kettle plus the mouth watering aroma are great for sales. If you are just getting started or just want a simpler method to get into the popcorn business, just go to Sam's Club or another big box store and purchase something like Act II Butter Lovers Microwave Popcorn (3oz., 30 bags per box). Individual servings cost about twenty five cents. Pop it in the microwave and it cooks to perfection in about three minutes.

If you expect large crowds, you should have several microwaves in operation to keep up with demand. Luckily, microwaves are pretty cheap these days. You can buy several of them for the cost of a professional popcorn popper. Microwave popcorn can also be served in the bag it was cooked in - saving you more money and work. Even if you use pre-buttered, pre-seasoned microwave popcorn, you should have plenty of popcorn salt available for customers to add. The saltier the popcorn, the better your drink sales will be. Movie theaters have known this for years!

3. Soft drinks - Be aware of local taste preferences when determining what type of soft drinks to sell. Don't automatically assume that everyone else shares your personal taste in beverages. At one concession stand that I visited, the operator was on a diet. Predictably, the only soft drinks available were diet soft drinks. I have sold canned drinks, used pre-mix with a soda fountain, and used two liter bottles to pour drinks from. They all have their place. Notice the prices at movie theaters. They provide a huge drink but charge a lot for it. It is not uncommon for a soft drink to cost you four dollars or more at the movie. Even at a restaurant, soft drinks are two to three dollars each. My advice is to use at least twenty ounce cups to create perception of value and then charge two dollars. Your prices are cheaper than the movies, in line with fast food restaurants, and still make more than a dollar fifty on each sale. If you plan to use canned drinks, you save money on ice and cups but should charge less for each one. You can charge one dollar for them and still more than double your money on them. Remember that the best profits involve a little more effort. If you sell your product in a cup with ice, you can get more for it.

4. Cheese Nachos - With a Sam's Club or other big box store near almost everyone, it is now easier than ever to operate a concession stand. You can buy cans of nacho cheese, huge bags of chips, and even standardized serving containers there. Put it all together and you have another product you can sell for two to three dollars each while keeping your cost around fifty cents. Cheese nachos have become a standard item at concession stands over the past few years. Why? People love them and the profit margin is huge. That's why movie theaters sell them. Don't be left out!

5. Snack cakes or other desert items - Technically, you are not supposed to do what I am about to outline. There is no health related reason not to do it. It is a safe and sanitary idea. Certain squeaky wheels in modern society who want to blame

everything on someone else decided that all packaged food available for human consumption should have a list of ingredients with percentages of each and calories per serving included. This applies to individual items but not to boxes of the exact same item. For example, you can buy an individually wrapped Little Debbie snack cake off the shelf in most convenience stores and it has all the required data printed on the back of the wrapping. If you buy a box of the same product, the box has the data printed on it but the individual items do not. For that reason, you are not supposed to break open a box and sell them individually. In spite of that legal disclaimer, I can honestly say that I have never seen any club have a problem who did exactly that. Even at wholesale prices, the individually wrapped items cost about twice as much as the same item in a box with several others. In the past, I have seen snack cakes, peanut butter crackers, cheese crackers, various chips, and even ice cream purchased in bulk boxes intended for home use, sold individually at fund raising events. The profit margin is bigger and the products are safe and sanitary. I'm just laying out potential items you can make the most profit selling at your club or organizations concession stand. You make the call.

Over the years I have refined the items that I use in my own snack bars and found that the items I listed above are a good product mix, simple to serve, and yield a good profit margin for my club. On some special occasions I might add sliced watermelon, pizza slices, or hamburgers to my menu. I only add any of these items if it is a special event and it makes good sense to do so. Every item you add to your menu makes your labor force larger and more skill is required. I try to make my concession stand operation as fool proof and simple as possible. All prices should be easy to add up since you probably won't be using a cash register to do it for you. Create a price structure that only requires you to keep quarters to make change with. Try your best to work it out where even quarters are not needed often. Dollars add up faster and they are easier for everyone concerned to deal with.

A well operated concession stand performs a community service and makes your organization some money. Don't try to be cheap. Serve good quality products. Have generous portion sizes. Provide the condiments required to make your products tastier. Don't charge too much but don't give it away either. Prices too cheap will make people think something is wrong with what you are selling. Perception of value, quality ingredients, and great customer service is key to successful operation of a concession stand. While this seems like a very conservative fund raiser, if operated within the guidelines described above, it can be a steady, long term money maker for your club.

ORGANIZATION EVENT P&L SHEET

Organization_____

Event_____

Date_____ Location_____

RECEIPTS:

    Total Food Sales   Gross Sales_____

    Total Cost of Food sold   Total Cost_____

    Total Cost of Paper Goods and Condiments   Total Cost_____

                                         TOTAL NET SALES_____

    Other Cash Receipts   _____

    Other Cash Receipts   _____

    Other Cash Receipts   _____

                 TOTAL CASH RECEIPTS FOR EVENT_____

EXPENSES:

Rent_____
Labor_____
Printing_____
Advertising_____
License_____
_____
_____
_____
_____
_____
_____

                                                   TOTAL EXPENSES_____

Total Receipts minus Expenses =   NET PROFIT_____

PROJECT EVALUATION

PROJECT TITLE _____

DATE HELD _____ LOCATION _____

TOTAL REVENUE $_____

TOTAL EXPENSES $_____

NET PROFIT $_____

Problems that should corrected:
_____
_____
_____
_____
_____
_____
_____
_____

Project Summary:
_____
_____
_____
_____
_____
_____
_____
_____

Project Chairperson _____

Signature _____

Date _____

Automobile Party

Throw an automobile party and generate thousands of dollars for your club.

The automobile party is a good example of a high risk/high return venture. Your organization's initial investment will be high but you can net over ten thousand dollars to support your club's other community projects.

For several years the Automobile Party was the favorite big money fund raiser of many charitable organizations. That was in the days when you could buy a pretty nice new car for around ten thousand dollars. Sometimes you could even get a dealer to donate a car or sell you a new car at actual cost, saving you even more money. Those days are pretty much over. You can still have a successful Automobile Party but you have to think outside the box when selecting your main prize. A classic dune buggy, restored pickup truck, or even a new motorcycle may be just the prize that makes your Automobile Party a success. I have seen each of these three suggested prizes successfully replace the brand new car of twenty five years ago. The prize you offer is limited only by your imagination and pocket book. The key is perception of value. I have even seen the main prized listed as simply $10,000! The more the prize looks like it is worth, the better. The mechanics of this fund raiser are very similar to the Generic 300 Club promotion.

I call this idea the Automobile Party because it originated with a new car as the main prize. The name is not as important as the concept. It is only a label to describe what can still be one of the best fund raising ideas around today. The big prize offered combined with a spectacular program will appeal to a wide spectrum of contributors.

The greater the number of members actively involved in this fund raising effort, the easier it will be to achieve your goal of raising a lot of money for your club. Organizations with a small, active membership will probably have a difficult time with this project. Although I have seen this plan work with only a few members doing all the work, I really don't recommend it. Those members had to dedicate every waking hour for several weeks to make this project a success. After they did it once, they swore they would never do it again.

By breaking up the overall project into specialized tasks, you make it much simpler for each chairman to handle. The selection of a sales chairman, banquet chairman, and promotions chairman should be accomplished as early in the process as possible. They will need all the time they can get to be able to do a good job at their assigned task.

The sales chairman must plan a campaign which will result in the sale of the planned number of tickets. To better reach your sales goal, the chairman should divide the available sales force into teams. These teams should include some "old hands" as well as some people with limited experience. Give each team a few good leads, such as individual names or business concerns which have supported your organization in the past. It makes it easier to make sales when your sales force has confidence. A few easy sales early in the campaign can make a big difference in your team's attitude and eventual success or failure.

A useful sales technique is to show a business what its competition is doing. In a smaller community, they will not want to be the only business which does not support a worthwhile community project. When I was editor of a small magazine, I would sometimes give free advertising to one business in a mall or shopping plaza. I then gave copies of the magazine to every business in the area. When they saw the first business advertising in my magazine, they asked how much it would cost for them to be in the next edition. Advertising sales rose 800% in just one month and remained high as long as I was there. You can use a similar technique to inspire local business to support your events. Make a brochure that shows them the recognition their business will receive. More importantly, include pictures of the annual banquet where you recognized contributors from the year before. As they say, a picture is worth a thousand words.

The promotions chairman must spread the word about your organization, what it does for the community, and information about your current fund raising program. Sometimes telling what you are going to do with the money is more important than what the actual project is. For example, I have known people who will sponsor anything that benefits veterans. They don't really care what you are doing today as long as it eventually benefits veterans. A lot of people feel the same way about schools, local sports teams, underprivileged children and so forth. The greater the visibility of your organization in the local community, the easier time your sales force will have in meeting their sales goals. Enhanced name recognition based on your clubs contributions to your community will add to your ability to improve your fiscal bottom line. By all means you should make money on your fund raising projects but you should always invest the proceeds in your local community.

If at all possible, get a popular local personality to be the spokesperson for your group. Take advantage of any positive means of spreading the word about your group and what it is doing for your community. Don't be afraid to list past contributions as well as your future plans. Through the efforts of a good publicity chairman, you increase public awareness of your efforts and increase the chances of receiving community support for your project.

To begin this project, you must secure 300 sequentially numbered tickets. Although you could probably sell more than 300 tickets in some areas, just about any community large enough to have civic organizations can support sales in this range. If you are developing a program for a really large school or community and feel that you can sell more than 300 tickets, then by all means expand the number to 400, 500 or even more. You just can't change the parameters during a sale. The principles for running a successful project remain the same.

The members of your organization must approach interested members of your community and sell chances to win the big prize for one hundred dollars each. I stress the word <u>interested</u> because it simply makes sense to try to sell chances to interested parties. Interested parties will share a common bond. They may be interested in supporting their football team, school band, or any worthwhile community project.

A quick calculation shows that once you sell three hundred chances for $100 each, you will have $30,000 in the bank. The question is, "What do the contributors receive for their $100?" The first thing each contributor receives is the chance to turn that $100 into $200! Americans are very fond of a chance to turn $100 into $200 so this alone may be enough motivation to help you sell your three hundred tickets. Once you have sold all your tickets, you can begin to have one drawing per week for a specified period of time, and award a $200 prize each time. You set the number of weeks that you want to do this. The longer the period, the more winners you have and the more it costs you. This accomplishes several purposes. First of all, it keeps your club on the minds of its contributors for a longer period of time. That makes it easier to sell chances in future years. Next, it offers contributors the opportunity to support a noble cause while having the potential to double their initial investment. The psychological impact of awarding crisp, new $100 bills as prizes is not to be overlooked. These drawings are in addition to drawings held at the banquet where you give away the big prize. Winning a weekly prize does not eliminate you from winning the big prize at the annual banquet. You can win a weekly prize and still win big at the banquet!

Your organization should also sponsor at least three $1,000 scholarships to deserving graduates of local high schools. These could include an athletic scholarship, band scholarship, and an actual academic scholarship. These three types of scholarships were recommended because each has a devoted base of community support for the programs they represent. In many communities, the most devoted of these groups is the band boosters. Even if the band boosters are not as active as some other groups, usually the band has more members than the other groups. When selecting the graduates to award scholarships, it is important that you involve the community by asking them for nominations. You could also include members of each booster organization on the selection committee. To gain status for your scholarship effort, make it a rule that your scholarship will go to someone that did not receive other monetary scholarships. Do not allow your scholarship to go to someone who applies for everything and ends up with several awards. You may even decide to award six, $500 scholarships so more people receive assistance. The local community will appreciate you spreading the wealth this way.

Once a year, you should put on an event where you give away the big prize. Each contributor should be allowed one guest at the event. When you send out invitations, you should require that they RSVP so you can get a good head count in advance. That helps you make sure you have enough food on hand and helps you keep costs down. You can't automatically assume that three hundred contributors plus one guest each will show up. Planning to feed six hundred people when only two hundred to two hundred fifty show up can be a costly mistake.

I have seen clubs spend all the money generated by their project and not put any in their general operating budget. It may be your goal to have a huge banquet style event and just break even overall. If that is your goal, then that is perfectly all right. A program that gives away $200 per week for several weeks; $3,000 worth of scholarships; and a huge night of entertainment and food; while paying for itself, is a great win for your organization and community. On the other hand, you can easily hire a decent local band, provide a great array of finger food and drinks and still keep a lot of money for your organization. It's really up to you and what your club decides it wants to do. Just gear your entertainment and food selections to the taste of your contributors. Just because you like a certain type music or food, it doesn't mean that everyone likes the same thing.

During the evening's entertainment, you will have other opportunities to make a few bucks. Fifty/fifty drawings are pretty common at these events. Any time you get a large group together, a drawing of this type is popular. Buy a double roll of numbered tickets and sell each ticket for $1. The more tickets you sell, the bigger the prize is and the more money the club makes. At one small event I recently attended, the fifty/fifty drawing earned the club a couple of hundred dollars and made one attendee very happy! You can also sell chances to win a vacation, shotgun, or other prizes to be given away during the night. This satisfies a craving to gamble that a lot of people seem to have. They also know that they are contributing to a good cause even if they don't win. Try your best to get your raffle items donated or at least purchase them at a deep discount. Don't make the mistake of buying a high dollar item that requires too many $1 sales just to cover the purchase price. While it should be fun for everyone, you must remember to leave your organization a good chance at making a profit. Don't forget to award the scholarships at this event so that you get even more community visibility for your efforts.

If you follow these steps, your organization can earn several thousand dollars. Look at the financial breakdown below.

>Income - 300 chances at $100 each equals $30,000.
>
>Expense - Tickets, food, and entertainment (depends on your clubs goal); $200 weekly drawings times number of weeks chosen (depends on your clubs goal).
>
>Scholarships - $3,000 worth of scholarships. Three scholarships for $1,000 each or six scholarships for $500. You decide on a suitable scholarship program.
>
>NET PROFIT: You can easily earn more than $10,000 if you follow my recommendations but do no worse than break even. Plus you get a great annual event.

As you can see, this fund raising idea can be tailored to your situation. You can easily expand the number of chances from 300 to 400 or even 500! You just can't change the number once you start. People want to know what their odds are up front so you can't change the parameters once the sale begins. Chances for $100 each have been successfully sold for more than twenty five years now. If your club is in an affluent neighborhood, you might try to sell them for $150 each. That's a judgment call you have to make. If your only purpose is funding scholarships, you can increase the number granted or the dollar amount of each scholarship. It's all up to you! If you don't think that your community will be excited about supporting scholarships, then reduce or eliminate them from your plan. Just substitute something the community will support.

You might want to put on a big banquet type event with steak or chicken available as choices for the main course. It will cost more but that doesn't matter if that is what you planned. This project is really easy to adjust to meet your local needs and has proven to be effective. If you need a big fund raising idea the Automobile Party could be the one for you. Remember that your organizations reputation is on the line. Everything you do must be seen to be fair and above board. I have included a set of rules that will eliminate many problems if you just follow them.

1. All numbers must be drawn in plain sight.

2. The last number drawn wins the grand prize.

3. The first number drawn wins at least $100. (If that is the ticket price.)

4. The drawing will continue, uninterrupted, until 289 more numbers have been drawn. Place these numbers in a consolation prize drum. From this drum, draw nineteen numbers. These numbers also win $100 each. This is the simplest way to do it and it will keep people from leaving early, once their number is drawn. They will stay because they know they still have a chance to win something. $2,000 will be given away during this phase.

5. By now, 290 numbers have been drawn. At this time, the owners of the last ten tickets will have the option of auctioning off their tickets or keeping them. Since one of the ten tickets will win the grand prize, people will bid on them to improve their chances of winning. Each ticket in the remaining ten may be bid on only once during this bid period. You cannot bid on a ticket then put it back up for bid immediately. After the first auction, you continue drawing numbers. If a number is still in play, you can put it up for bids again when there are five tickets remaining and you allow another auction.

6. Tickets must be presented to club officials for inclusion in the auctions.

7. Tickets will be auctioned in the order that they were presented to club officials for auction.

8. Bidding typically starts at $100 and rises until the last bid is received.

9. There is no maximum bid.

10. The owner has the right to refuse all bids or they may set a minimum. You may decide to change this rule to say once bidding starts, the ticket will be sold.

I have seen it both ways and both seem to work as long as it's clear from the beginning exactly what the rule is.

11. The proceeds of each accepted bid will be split with ninety percent going to the owner and ten percent to the club. This keeps it interesting and makes you money!

12. Tickets purchased at auction must be paid for immediately. No more drawings will be held until the auction is totally closed out and tickets paid for.

13. All checks will be made payable to the club and the club will guarantee payment to the original owner of the ticket.

14. When there are only ten tickets left, you will allow the owners another chance to sell them at auction. Same rules apply as before. You may want to hold another auction when there are only three tickets left. As the main prize gets closer, the value of the remaining tickets usually grows exponentially.

15. You should have some nice consolation prizes for the owners of the last ten tickets. As each one is drawn and the odds of winning the grand prize increase, so should the value of the consolation prize.

16. The owner of the 299th ticket drawn should win at least $1000.

17. The winner of the grand prize (unless it is cash) has the option of auctioning off the prize with ten percent going to the club.

18. All rules must be agreed upon and available for everyone to see before the first ticket is sold. Any disputes concerning the drawing or auctions will be settled by the club committee.

As you can see, the club will make even more money during the drawing. I have seen people bid $5000 during the last ticket auction and even more if the grand prize is on the auction block. The club's ten percent can add up pretty quickly!

This project can provide a relatively large net profit for your organization to use on other community projects. Once your community sees the results of successful execution of the Automobile Party, you will see your fund raising problems evaporate. People will ask you if it is time yet to buy chances for next year's give away.

ORGANIZATION EVENT P&L SHEET

Organization_____

Event_____

Date_____**Location**_____

RECEIPTS:

    Total Number of Tickets Sold @ $_____ Gross Sales_____

    Total Number of Tickets Sold @ $_____ Gross Sales_____

    Total Number of Tickets Sold @ $_____ Gross Sales_____

                      TOTAL TICKET GROSS SALES_____

    Other Cash Receipts   _____

    Other Cash Receipts   _____

    Other Cash Receipts   _____

                    TOTAL CASH RECEIPTS FOR EVENT_____

EXPENSES:

Rent_____
Labor_____
Printing_____
Advertising_____
License_____
_____
_____
_____
_____
_____
_____

                                      TOTAL EXPENSES_____

Total Receipts minus Expenses =   NET PROFIT_____

PROJECT EVALUATION

PROJECT TITLE _____

DATE HELD_____LOCATION_____

TOTAL REVENUE $_____

TOTAL EXPENSES $_____

NET PROFIT $_____

Problems that should corrected:
_____
_____
_____
_____
_____
_____
_____
_____
_____

Project Summary:
_____
_____
_____
_____
_____
_____
_____
_____
_____

Project Chairperson_____

Signature_____

Date_____

Concert Promotions

Bring in popular, professional entertainment and make money with careful planning and a little effort.

One or two of your club members can successfully coordinate a concert. Most of the details should be taken care of by professionals hired by your club. This increases the cost but assures that you will have a professionally presented show.

Concert promotions seem to be pretty straight forward. You select a group, hire them to perform, then stand back and count your money. Right? Not exactly. Before you can even think about putting on a concert, there is a lot of local research you need to do. Here are some of the variables to consider before you decide to promote a concert in your area.

One of the first considerations is whether anyone else is already promoting concerts in your area. If a promoter is regularly offering concerts then yours might just be one too many. That is a quick way to lose money. Even if someone else occasionally puts on concerts in your area you must be aware of them so you don't schedule an event too close to their date. Even worse, you might schedule one on the same date. In one local community close to me, two different organizations put on a concert on the same night. That would be bad enough but they both had "The Temptations" performing. If you know anything about the business, you know that there have been many members of the "Temptations" over the years. At any given time, there may be two or more groups calling themselves "The Temptations" and putting on shows across America. Each group has one member of what most consider the real "Temptations" performing with an otherwise all new lineup.

That brings to mind something else you should worry about. As the older groups age, more and more of the original members are being replaced by younger performers. You think you are booking the originals and there could be only one original (if that many). If your ticket buyers think you are trying to deceive them things can go bad fast!

Another reason to worry about other promoters is that there may only be one venue in your town large enough to hold a successful concert. The band you want to present might only be available on a date that the venue is already in use. Even if you can get the venue for the date you want, another promoter could schedule something close enough to your date to ruin your chances for success. In many communities, there is just not enough extra money floating around for everyone to succeed as a concert promoter.

If no one else is promoting concerts in your area you still need to take into consideration other events like the Super Bowl, World Series, College Football, local High School games and events, and so on. For the best chance of success, you want to promote a show when nothing else is going on.

Next you should find out about the hidden costs of putting on a concert. Most people will consider building rental but forget about event insurance or security costs. Even a one night event will cost at least four hundred dollars for insurance but maybe more. Some venues require you to only use off duty police officers for security. They dictate how many you must hire, what you must pay them, how many hours you have to pay for, and worst of all, what the security will do for you. In one venue I used, the police would only sit in the box office. No parking lot patrols. No venue walk through. No crowd control. If someone tried to rob the box office they might have done something to earn the money I was required to pay them. The absolute worst part was that I was required to pay them twice their normal salary to do nothing. Some venues keep all revenue from concessions plus the rental fee you pay for the use of the facility. They may even tack on a set up fee if you want chairs lined up a certain way. If you run into this kind of local "support" it's better not to even try to run an event there. I have also run events in venues that were wonderful to work with. They did everything they could to be of assistance and were totally reasonable in their pricing. I just want you to be aware of what could happen if you don't ask the right questions up front.

In the concert business there is something called a "routing" date. Always check for routing when negotiating for an act for your concert. Sometimes a band will be playing in a nearby large city and need something to do between bigger dates. That is where the routing date comes in. If your town happens to be on the way from one big date to another, you may get a substantial discount. A band on tour incurs expenses every day whether they are working or not. That means that in many cases they would rather play for less than sit around doing nothing. It's just common sense that you can get a performer to play for less if you are somewhat flexible on the date.

Choosing an act that will sell tickets is not easy. Today's performers seem to believe that they are worth a huge amount of money if they get even one song on the charts. These little known acts usually don't have a dedicated following yet so promoting a concert with them can be a hit or miss proposition. Remember too that just because you like a certain entertainer or group, that does not mean that everyone does. I personally enjoy the music of Jose Feliciano, but in my neighborhood I couldn't sell ten tickets to see him.

Something else to consider is community resistance to a local group promoting concerts. What I mean by this is actually pretty simple. I have seen "tribute bands" in

Las Vegas or at other tourist destinations get away with charging forty to fifty dollars per ticket. Most shows are close to sold out. Yet I have seen locals balk at paying twenty dollars a ticket when you bring a similar group to the local venue. There are people who believe that if a local group is putting a show on, it can't be good. Many people also believe that a reasonably priced show can't be a good show. Perception of value is important so don't price your tickets too cheap and be sure to advertise the big venues your band has played in.

I put on a low budget show for an American Legion Post a couple of years ago. It featured a Johnny Cash Tribute Artist, Buddy Holly Tribute Artist, and an Elvis Tribute Artist. The Elvis Act came from Branson, MO where he performed six days a week for about three years before moving to the Memphis area. A show like this one would cost at least thirty five to forty five dollars per ticket in Branson or Las Vegas. We sold tickets for twenty dollars each. You can guess the results. The American Legion Post sold about one hundred and fifty tickets. After paying for the venue and the talent, they still cleared about eight hundred dollars but it should have been lots more. Whatever you do, do not use a local Tribute Artist and expect to make money. No matter how good they are or what a crowd they draw in other cities, everyone will know them as "Joe the Plumber" or something similar in that local community. There are literally hundreds of Elvis Tribute Artists working in America today. Some are really good and some are pathetic. If your target audience is fifty years and older, a good Elvis Tribute who drives in from somewhere far away, will usually make you money. By the same token, Beatles Tribute Acts are much more rare and usually cost a lot more to book. A really good Beatles Tribute recently played near me and sold out a twelve hundred seat venue. Tickets were forty five dollars and up! That group cost about twenty five thousand dollars for the one show but it turned out to be worth it. Many twenty five thousand dollar acts available today are not. My point is that picking a group who will be successful is not easy. If it was, everybody would do it.

If you just need to generate one thousand dollars or so, you can usually get away with using a low cost local act. To make it work, you have to package it as an event, not a concert. For example you can call your event a "Cookout" or "Hotdog Dinner" or something similar. You package a meal with live music. Keep the food cost down and use a respected local act and you can easily clear a thousand or more dollars. When you do this type event, you have to tie the event to a specific fund raising project. If you want to raise funds to buy uniforms for your baseball team, then you say so in your advertising. That way the main focus is uniforms for the team, not the concert. The concert and food are just an excuse for people to get together and support the team and help with the uniform purchase. Substitute any worthy cause and the project works exactly the same way. Obviously, this smaller scale concert idea is a less risk, less reward venture but it has a high chance for success.

Always try to get co-sponsors for any level of concert. If you are featuring a national act, then you may be able to get sponsorship from local businesses. The most targeted businesses are auto dealerships and radio stations. I have said it before but it's worth repeating. Don't go into a radio station expecting them to advertise your show for free. If they do it for one group, every group will expect the same treatment. They may offer you a discount or a radio personality to host the event but normally won't just give you free advertising. The old days of radio depending on local good will and wanting to be seen as a force for good in the local community are largely over. Most radio stations are part of national chains now and are run by large corporations. The old days of mom and pop radio stations are gone. Most large auto dealerships use advertising agencies these days so you usually have to deal with the agency instead of the dealership. You also have to get in sync with their advertising and budget cycle. They usually have an annual plan with specific dates and deadlines for planning the months ahead. Miss the deadline and you can't get any sponsorship consideration until next year. Most civic organizations just don't plan that far ahead.

Don't waste your advertising money. Concerts generally don't get good results from print advertising. Most of the younger people that go to concerts do not read the newspaper anymore. Years ago, you couldn't have a successful event without advertising in the local newspaper. Today, that is not the case. If your local paper has an entertainment insert that lists local events that comes out once a week, that might be worth advertising in. The Memphis newspaper publishes an insert on Saturdays that lists concerts, festivals, fairs, shows and other entertainment that will be available that week. Even then, you need to either go with a large ad or don't bother. People just don't notice the small printed ads that have no pictures like they used to.

Social media like Facebook, Twitter, and so on seems to be the modern replacement for newspaper ads. You can create a website or Facebook page for your event. You still have to know how to drive people to those sites. Just putting information up there is not enough. Email blasts worked for awhile but many people have their spam filter set so that many of these automatically go into their junk file now. Social media is always evolving so what I write about today could be obsolete in a couple of years. While working as the Director of the United States Navy's National Advertising Program for Navy Recruiting, I used to do something very simple to find out what social media was relevant at any time. I just asked people who were the same age as my target audience where and how they preferred to get information. That concept works now and will continue to work as long as there are people. To find out if my advertising worked, I constantly asked people where they heard about Navy opportunities. That way I knew if I was advertising in the right places and in the right way. You can do the same thing to make your advertising for local events more effective. Just because you get your information a certain way, don't automatically assume that everyone else does as well. Each generation has its own preferences. Ignore that at your peril.

My last advice for any type concert or event is to be professional. Start on time. Deliver what you advertised. Give a good value for the ticket price. Make sure you have a good sound and lighting check before the audience gets there. Pay attention to the details and you can have a very successful fund raising project that will not only make money but will let your community know that you are a first class organization!

ORGANIZATION EVENT P&L SHEET

Organization_____

Event_____

Date_____**Location**_____

RECEIPTS:

Total Number of Tickets Sold @ $_____ Gross Sales_____

Total Number of Tickets Sold @ $_____ Gross Sales_____

Total Number of Tickets Sold @ $_____ Gross Sales_____

TOTAL TICKET GROSS SALES_____

Other Cash Receipts _____

Other Cash Receipts _____

Other Cash Receipts _____

TOTAL CASH RECEIPTS FOR EVENT_____

EXPENSES:

Rent_____
Labor_____
Printing_____
Advertising_____
License_____
Security_____
Talent_____
_____
_____
_____
_____

TOTAL EXPENSES_____

Total Receipts minus Expenses =   NET PROFIT_____

PROJECT EVALUATION

PROJECT TITLE _____

DATE HELD _____ LOCATION _____

TOTAL REVENUE $_____

TOTAL EXPENSES $_____

NET PROFIT $_____

Problems that should corrected:

_____
_____
_____
_____
_____
_____
_____
_____
_____
_____

Project Summary:

_____
_____
_____
_____
_____
_____
_____
_____
_____
_____

Project Chairperson_____

Signature_____

Date_____

Movie Premiers

This unique project can raise a lot of money and could be used at least once every year.

Good planning, hard work, and the cooperation of your local theater can make this project successful and fun for everyone. This is an idea that I have never used but included in the first edition of this book (1990). The plan was described to me by exploitation film great David F. Friedman. He swore that he successfully executed the project as outlined and made a lot of money for charity.

Almost every town in America has a movie theater. Although they are right under your nose, you probably never considered that they could be a potential source of revenue for your organization. Hosting a movie premiere can earn a lot of money with good planning and a well coordinated effort.

After your committee is formed and you decide to try this project, you must reach an agreement with the local theater. A locally owned and operated theater is your best choice if you want this to work. National chains are harder to deal with like every other nationally based business. Since they have no local roots, they usually care less about your community other than as a place to make money for themselves. The way this works is your organization sponsors a special, one performance only, premiere showing of a particular film. It should be shown the night before the film begins its regular run. Your organization will pay the theater their regular admission price for every person attending the showing. Because it's a charity event and an exclusive showing, your organization will print special tickets and charge double or triple the normal admission. Most theaters require a minimum customer guarantee before they will consider supporting an event like this. If you reach a deal for eight dollar tickets and charge twenty dollars per ticket, you stand to make an excellent profit. The theater gains a crowd on what would have been a slow weeknight and increased sales in their concession stand. The theater will make more money on concession sales than the actual movie. Consider that you sell two hundred tickets to your event. Two hundred times twenty dollars is four thousand dollars gross sales. You will owe the theater two hundred tickets at eight dollars each for a total of sixteen hundred dollars. That leaves a potential profit of twenty four hundred dollars for your club.

Try to pick a movie that lends itself to such a promotion. Pick a subject targeted towards a specific audience. If you are premiering a children's movie, you should go for double priced tickets and work the churches and businesses that cater to children in your area. Why businesses? Because they may purchase tickets in bulk numbers to use as promotional giveaways in their stores or to reward loyal customers. Auto dealerships might give away a pair of tickets to anyone who takes a test drive on a certain day. Furniture stores might give a pair of tickets to anyone who finances their purchase through the store credit department. The way that these tickets can be used to support local business is limited only by the imagination. Don't waste your time trying to sell these tickets at school. Kids are a hard sell. Go directly to parents and others involved in that market. It's better to promote films with broader audience appeal. With the right movie you can almost triple the original ticket price and increase your profit margin. Imagine if you could have done this with a big Star Wars, Star Trek, Hunger Games, Harry Potter type film. Tickets to an early premiere would almost sell themselves. Especially if you make the movie going experience an event and not just a movie.

There are two ways to handle the actual staging of the event. One is to try to create a Hollywood Premiere atmosphere. Have light hors d'oeuvres in the lobby before the show. Arrange for valet parking to be available. Make it a dress up affair. Either dress up in nicer clothes than you normally wear to the movie or dress up like the characters in the movie! Think Rocky Horror or a Steampunk event. Try to get a local celebrity to serve as master of ceremonies. Include drawings for door prizes to add a special quality to your event. Surround your event with excitement. If you do this event well, people will put it on their calendar and look forward to it each year. Do it too often and the novelty wears off.

There are companies that make a living doing direct telephone solicitations. They put several people in a room filled with telephones. They give them a script to work from and a list of local phone numbers then stand back and watch them work. I personally will not use these guys but I have seen them be very successful at selling tickets. One Jaycee Chapter I was in used a professional group to sell tickets to a low budget show in the City Auditorium. They actually sold more than fourteen hundred tickets. We were very concerned since the Auditorium only seated eight hundred! Lucky for us, many of the purchasers never showed up. Some businesses had purchased fifty to one hundred ticket blocks and gave them to their customers. Since the customers did not pay for them, they felt no great drive to actually go to the show. I recommend that if you try this or any variation on the theme of promoting a "movie day" that you make it as spectacular as possible and handle ticket sales personally. I have seen big churches buy out a particular showing of a movie, then sell the seats to members of their congregation. They usually add a few bucks to the ticket price so they make money on the deal. The real key to this event is to make it special. Let people know what the money is being raised for and let them in on the results.

Don't forget to advertise your event. This or any other fund raising project you choose to put on should not be a secret. Just remember that you have to advertise if you want to be successful! I've covered ways to advertise on other projects so I won't repeat the information here.

ORGANIZATION EVENT P&L SHEET

Organization_____

Event_____

Date_____**Location**_____

RECEIPTS:

Total Number of Tickets Sold @ $_____ Gross Sales_____

Total Number of Tickets Sold @ $_____ Gross Sales_____

Total Number of Tickets Sold @ $_____ Gross Sales_____

TOTAL TICKET GROSS SALES_____

Other Cash Receipts _____

Other Cash Receipts _____

Other Cash Receipts _____

TOTAL CASH RECEIPTS FOR EVENT_____

EXPENSES:

Rent_____
Labor_____
Printing_____
Advertising_____
License_____
Security_____
Talent_____
_____
_____
_____
_____

TOTAL EXPENSES_____

Total Receipts minus Expenses =   NET PROFIT_____

PROJECT EVALUATION

PROJECT TITLE _____

DATE HELD_____LOCATION_____

TOTAL REVENUE $_____

TOTAL EXPENSES $_____

NET PROFIT $_____

Problems that should corrected:
_____
_____
_____
_____
_____
_____
_____
_____
_____

Project Summary:
_____
_____
_____
_____
_____
_____
_____
_____
_____

Project Chairperson_____

Signature_____

Date_____

Auctions

A well run auction can earn a lot of money for your organization, with little to no investment. Especially if most of the items are donated!

Auctions offer you the opportunity to turn one man's junk into another man's treasure. All while making money for your organization!

I found out about auctions almost by accident, when I helped close an Army recreation center that had been in operation since the early 1940's. The lady in charge of operations had apparently never thrown anything away in the last fifty years! At first glance it looked like there would be several truck loads delivered to the local dump. Instead, I decided to hold an auction and see what kind of money we could make from all the old stuff in the building. Instead of having to pay someone to clean out the building and haul items away, we held an auction on site and made an unexpected amount of money. The auction grossed over sixteen thousand dollars. The only expense was about one hundred dollars for an advertisement in the local paper. The advertisement was placed in the "auctions" section of the classifieds. The results were phenomenal. Over three hundred people came to the auction and almost everyone purchased something!

Here's how it works. First, sort through the items and haul away the real trash. Line up all the sellable items in rows so that customers can easily see them. Next, tag all the items with a lot number. These lot numbers should be listed on a handout for each prospective bidder. As individuals sign up for their personal bid numbers, give them a copy of the itemized listing. This helps them decide how much to bid on each items and lets them know when each item is coming up for auction.

The day before the auction, allow prospective bidders to view the items to be auctioned. This time is allotted so bidders can see if the items work or not. On auction day, once bidding starts, all items are off limits to bidders. Watch out because unscrupulous bidders may try to move items from one lot to another without your knowledge. Anticipate this problem and you can easily stop it from happening.

Start the auction on time. If you say the auction begins at nine o'clock, then you should start promptly at nine o'clock. Establish control of the event early. Read the rules of the auction to your bidders before you begin bidding. The rules should answer many common questions concerning your action. Include when and how they must pay for items they buy. Are checks acceptable or only cash? When must items be removed from the premises? What is the minimum bid increment that you will allow? Can I get away with raising the bid by a penny, a nickel, a dime, a quarter, half dollar, dollar or even higher increments? Be specific on each item. By answering many of these questions before you begin, you will avoid time consuming problems later on. My first auction listed over three hundred and fifty items and took about six hours to complete bidding. This was way too long! After that auction, I began all auctions at nine a.m. and completed them in around three hours. That time frame also allows you to sell drinks and pastries if you have enough people left over to run a concession stand.

The key to success is to make the auction quick, comfortable, convenient, and interesting. Sometimes a little showmanship helps increase the amount you receive for an item. I was selling a ten year old welding machine and the bidding stalled out at one hundred dollars. I told the bidders how they could buy the welder and some scrap steel we were also selling. They could then build their wives some child proof furniture. The bidding picked up and the old welder sold for two hundred sixty five dollars! That was actually more than it cost new, ten years before! As you can see, I usually perform as auctioneer at my auctions. I do not perform the auctioneer "babble" because I believe most people would rather clearly understand what is going on. I can't tell you how many times at an auction bidders lost money on an item simply because they didn't understand what was being said. The bidders are your prospective customers. You have to make it as easy for them to understand what is going on as possible. They really don't want to have to work to spend their money. Make it easy for them and they will usually spend a lot more.

After the auction, keep the new owners out of the area where the items are stored. Have some choke point where you can give the items to their new owners. I have seen some close calls when bidders were allowed to pick up their items on their own. People are basically honest, BUT you don't want to tempt them. Often bidders will disagree when they bid on the wrong item. They thought they were bidding on the new chair but they were actually bidding on an older one sitting beside it. They just got the numbers confused because the description was similar. That is why you must control every aspect of the auction site.

I found a treasure trove of sellable items by accident. You will probably have to work a little harder. Most of the items I sold could have easily ended up as more trash at the landfill. Instead, people paid a lot of money for them. Your club can build up items over a period of time then later hold an auction. You must have a free or very low cost storage area where you can accumulate auction stock. You can accept donations like refrigerators, stoves, appliances, tools, old campers, cars, trucks and so on. It really doesn't matter if they are operational or not. You just have to describe them honestly in your auction. Some people may be bidding because they want the items for parts. You need about one hundred major items to hold a good two to three hour auction. That should be your target.

Use the same methods as I described in the chapter on Rummage Sales to help accumulate auction items. Since I first experienced the excitement and revenue potential of an auction, I have never put on another Rummage Sale, only auctions.

As an added thought, if your organization has its own building that is roomy and in a decent location, you can also make money from auctions another way. In every town there are local auctions. There are also people who make their living buying things and taking them to auctions to sell them. If you can get in touch with the locals who are in this business you can organize an ongoing auction at your location. Normally the house (location) gets 10% of the gross, just for hosting the event. You can also put in a few of your own items and make all the money from the sale. In addition, you can run the concession stand and keep all profits from sales. When I was promoting professional wrestling, I had a large building with lots of room and about three hundred chairs in it so I also held auctions there. We did this one night each week from around Thanksgiving through Christmas. We dropped back to once or twice a month the rest of the year. The money I made from auctions actually paid monthly rent and utilities for the building so all the money I made from wrestling was pure profit. Be flexible in your thinking. It's almost always more rewarding that way!

ORGANIZATION EVENT P&L SHEET

Organization_____

Event_____

Date_____Location_____

RECEIPTS:

    Total Admission Tickets Sold @ $_____ Gross Sales_____

    Total Admission Tickets Sold @ $_____ Gross Sales_____

                       TOTAL TICKET GROSS SALES_____

    Other Cash Receipts (Concessions)   _____

    Other Cash Receipts (Raffles)   _____

    Other Cash Receipts   _____

                  TOTAL CASH RECEIPTS FOR EVENT_____

ITEM SOLD: BID AMOUNT:

_____
_____
_____
_____
_____
_____
_____
_____
_____
_____
_____
_____
_____
_____

EXPENSES:
Rent_____
Labor_____
Printing_____
Advertising_____
License_____
Security_____
Raffle items_____
Auctions items_____
_____
_____
_____
_____
_____
_____

                                        TOTAL EXPENSES_____

Total Receipts minus Expenses =   NET PROFIT_____

PROJECT EVALUATION

PROJECT TITLE _____

DATE HELD_____ LOCATION_____

TOTAL REVENUE $_____

TOTAL EXPENSES $_____

NET PROFIT $_____

Problems that should corrected:

_____
_____
_____
_____
_____
_____
_____
_____
_____

Project Summary:

_____
_____
_____
_____
_____
_____
_____
_____
_____

Project Chairperson_____

Signature_____

Date_____

Professional Wrestling

Provide inexpensive entertainment for the whole family and earn five hundred to thousands of dollars.

Professional wrestling can make a few hundred dollars with no risk to your organization. If you are willing to assume some risk, the sky is the limit!

Professional wrestling is sports entertainment which has had its ups and downs through the years. Some areas are totally saturated with local shows while other areas have not had a wrestling show for years. There was a time during the late eighties and early nineties when I worked on wrestling shows two or three times per week. Most of them were fund raisers for high school athletic programs, band boosters, or volunteer fire departments. There are two basic formats that promoters usually offer organizations as fund raisers. One is the straight percentage program and the other is the guarantee program. As you would suspect, the straight percentage program requires little to no risk by the local organization. The wrestling promoter will bring the entire show, ring, PA and announcer, wrestlers and referee and you just provide the location. Usually the high school gym or National Guard armory. The gate is split between the wrestling promotion and the local organization. Generally the split is seventy five percent for the wrestlers and twenty five percent for the locals. As a wrestling promoter, I never really liked this set up. The problem with it is simple. Some local organizations feel like they have completed a successful fund raiser when they clear one hundred dollars. Then they don't really try to increase their sales because they have already successfully raised one hundred dollars. That leaves the wrestling promotion with three hundred dollars. No promoter can put on a decent show for three hundred dollars. If the wrestling promoter loses money on the date, then they will never offer to run there again. Your organization made its hundred dollars once and burned a bridge to future income.

Another form of percentage deal, and the only one I'd ever sign up for as a wrestling promoter is this. The wrestling promoter gets the first X number of dollars through ticket sales and then they split everything above that with the local organization. The wrestling promoter and your organization work out what that amount will be before the percentage split begins. The promoter will want to cover his actual expenses for putting on the show and then depend on the percentage for his profit. Here is the tricky part. Most local people have no idea what professional wrestlers actually cost. A sneaky promoter will tell you that he must have the first fifteen hundred dollars to cover expenses when he actually only needs eight or nine hundred dollars to cover. Try to get advice from other groups who have used this wrestling organization. Make the wrestling promoter give you references so you can ask other groups how much money they earned and how they split ticket sales with the wrestling promoter. Actually, this split usually works out better for the local organization because they have to be committed to working hard so they will earn any money. The bigger the crowd in attendance, the more money the local organization earns off ticket sales and the all important concession stand. While your organization usually keeps all profits from the concession stand, the wrestlers usually keep all profits from selling souvenir pictures and personalized T shirts. Many of the wrestlers will earn more from souvenir sales than they earned for wrestling. Since you have a crowd together, don't forget to raffle off something during the intermission. It's fun and increases profits!

In every area where I have had personal experience in promoting wrestling shows, there are unscrupulous promoters that will offer you a slate of wrestlers at an incredibly low price. You get what you pay for. If the wrestlers work for little or nothing, they are usually worth little or nothing. That may allow you to make money once but it will also tarnish your organizations reputation in the community. It is not worth it! Only use reputable wrestling promoters. They will make a reasonable deal with you so both parties make money. If the deal sounds too good to be true, it probably is!

Most good local wrestling promotions can get one or two nationally known wrestlers to headline your show. That is plenty. Local or regional stars usually put on a better show than the national wrestlers so once the show begins, no one will question the lineup. The younger wrestlers will give the fans more than their money's worth. The wrestling business is in a constant state of flux with people gaining and losing national contracts almost weekly. For that reason alone, you will not want to advertise that certain wrestlers will appear at your show to be held three months from now. No one can be sure who will be available that far out. A preferred wrestler might get a new national contract or get injured so that he can't perform at your show. If the choice is between honoring a commitment to appear for a couple of hundred dollars at your show or go to World Wrestling Entertainment for hundreds of thousands of dollars, you can guess who is going to lose. It won't be something in the control of the local promoter either. Don't get mad at him when he has to change the lineup. It's just part of the way the business works.

Now for a few words of warning. I am spelling these out for wrestling but they really apply to any fund raising event you put on that depends on someone or some group outside your organization. Most wrestling promoters deal strictly in cash. They pay the wrestlers and other workers in cash so they will not want a check from your organization. Do not give them substantial cash advances or cash checks for them! Forewarned is forearmed! Insist on a contract that specifies in detail what each party will provide, and stick to it. Detail who provides and pays for the facility, posters, and promotional items, tickets, wrestling ring, referee, the announcer, crowd control (security), ticket sellers, ushers, event insurance, and even the public address system the announcer uses. These items often become bones of contention when dealing with less than professional organizations. The situation is usually exacerbated if the show doesn't do well and ticket sales are light! Suddenly everything and every cost becomes a point for discussion. Be sure to get references if you don't already know the promoter personally. Professional wrestling is not a bad event to stage. Just be businesslike and be careful. If your organization feels that it can work hard and sell a lot of tickets, then the best thing to do is buy out a show for around fifteen hundred dollars. That way you keep all the money after you recover the fifteen hundred dollars you spent on the show. If you aren't sure, then the percentage split is the best for you. Remember that a show offered to you for less than fifteen hundred dollars (and I've seen low budget promoters promise a show for five hundred dollars) you probably won't like what you end up with. They may try to pass off local wrestlers as national TV stars, hoping that you won't know the difference. Trust me. You will! The fans who attend will let you know about the deception and your organizations reputation will be severely tarnished.

Since a lot of the individual wrestlers' income is derived from selling souvenirs, they will usually be amenable to making public appearances to promote your show in the local area. We used to put on "Just Say No" and "Stay In School" programs at local schools during the day, as a means to promote that night's wrestling show. I've had wrestlers signing autographs at Walmart, the local grocery store, in schools, the local mall or shopping center. Any appearance that you can set up to bring positive attention to your show is a good thing to do.

There are two major mistakes that sponsors make in staging wrestling events. The most common is to pay too much money to the promoter for their first event. I saw an athletic booster club pay five thousand dollars plus fifty percent of the gross over the first five thousand dollars for a show that I could have put on for fifteen hundred dollars and still made a modest profit. They did this because they were uninformed. They thought that if they paid more, they would have a better show. That show actually grossed more than eight thousand dollars in ticket sales but after all expenses, the sponsor only made about six hundred dollars from ticket sales. The snack bar earned a lot more than that! After that experience, they don't even want to discuss wrestling as a fund raiser. Another unscrupulous promoter took ten thousand dollars from Toys for Tots for a guaranteed wrestling show. The lineup of wrestlers was actually extraordinary BUT the promoter was supposed to use the money to both pay for the wrestlers and advertise the show. He didn't advertise it at all. The result was that only about two hundred and fifty people showed up in a venue that seated more than ten thousand people. The crooked promoter gave the sponsor a stack of fake contracts showing where he paid one thousand dollars for a wrestler he actually paid three hundred dollars. Wrestlers that worked for seventy five dollars were listed on the phony contracts at three or four hundred dollars. You get the picture. It was disgraceful behavior on the part of the wrestler promoter. He disappeared with the money and gave legitimate wrestling promoters a black eye that they will never recover from in that area. Be careful!

The second major mistake that people make is to rely totally on free advertising. Every group thinks that their event is worthy of free public service announcements on local radio and TV. That is just not so these days! You want to make a profit from your event and the advertisers want some of that money too.

Professional wrestling as a fund raiser is unusual, provides inexpensive entertainment for the family, and can be put on at little to no risk for the sponsoring organization. By exercising good judgment you can sponsor an exciting event that everyone will enjoy and you will make some money for your organization.

ORGANIZATION EVENT P&L SHEET

Organization_____

Event_____

Date_____Location_____

RECEIPTS:

    Total Admission Tickets Sold @ $_____ Gross Sales_____

    Total Admission Tickets Sold @ $_____ Gross Sales_____

                  TOTAL TICKET GROSS SALES_____

    Other Cash Receipts (Concessions)   _____

    Other Cash Receipts (Raffles)   _____

    Other Cash Receipts   _____

                TOTAL CASH RECEIPTS FOR EVENT_____

ITEM SOLD: BID AMOUNT:

_____
_____
_____
_____
_____
_____
_____
_____
_____
_____
_____
_____
_____
_____

EXPENSES:
Rent_____
Labor_____
Printing_____
Advertising_____
License_____
Security_____
Raffle items_____
Auctions items_____
_____
_____
_____
_____
_____

                                          TOTAL EXPENSES_____

Total Receipts minus Expenses =   NET PROFIT_____

PROJECT EVALUATION

PROJECT TITLE _____

DATE HELD_____LOCATION_____

TOTAL REVENUE $_____

TOTAL EXPENSES $_____

NET PROFIT $_____

Problems that should corrected:
_____
_____
_____
_____
_____
_____
_____
_____
_____

Project Summary:
_____
_____
_____
_____
_____
_____
_____
_____
_____

Project Chairperson_____

Signature_____

Date_____

Pancake Breakfast

A simple way to earn a few hundred dollars and earn goodwill in your community.

Most people love to eat and pancakes are cheap and tasty! Well established pancake breakfasts are easy to put on and can earn a lot of money in a few hours. While I call this the "Pancake Breakfast" chapter, you can use exactly the same principles to successfully put on a Fish Fry, BBQ Dinner, Fried Chicken Dinner, or fill in with any other food item that is cheap to serve and attracts a broad audience. Don't forget Spaghetti. It's cheap, cheap, cheap!!!

An idea as simple as the pancake breakfast has been included for the first time in one of my books. Why? Because it is so simple that you may not think of it. Just this week I noticed a poster for a Kiwanis pancake breakfast to be held on Saturday. The poster was on the bulletin board of the Gold's Gym where I work out four times a week. A large percentage of the members at that particular gym are over forty years of age. All the talk was about the upcoming pancake breakfast. That made me think about all the pancake breakfasts that I have attended during my lifetime. Every one that I attended was an unqualified success even though they were put on by a wide range of organizations. Everyone from fire departments to athletic boosters to civic groups have successfully put on pancake breakfasts to earn a few bucks.

People seem to love pancakes when they don't eat them every day. Sure you can buy pancakes at many fast food restaurants today but people still want the feeling that they are serving the community as they buy and eat your pancakes. They realize that corporate pancakes from a national chain are not doing the local community any good. They just take your money and send it back up the line to corporate headquarters. Your pancakes not only fill the belly, they earn money that will do something good for your community. Don't forget to let people know what the money you hope to raise will be used for. Put out a big jar for donations somewhere near the place where people pay for their meal. They might just put their change in the jar if they like what you plan to do with the money! Every little bit helps.

First of all, pancakes cost very little to make. That's why a lot of chains that feature breakfast food will offer you unlimited pancakes. They want you to be overstuffed when you leave so you think you got good value for your money. Trust me; breakfast food is the lowest cost food you can sell. The only thing you must remember is this. Offer unlimited pancakes at your breakfast but limit the amount of bacon, sausage, or other side meat you offer with them. While pancakes are very cheap, you can lose all your profit if the customers take too much meat to go with them. Offer one or two pieces of sausage or two or three slices of bacon with the pancakes. That is a generous portion and is a fairly standard amount that is served in commercial restaurants. Only the pancakes are unlimited. Remember also that pancakes are very filling. It's almost impossible to eat so many pancakes that you lose money on the deal.

Just like all my projects, I recommend that you start on time and be ready to serve when the first customer comes in. Let the customer pay first so that is out of the way before they are served and before they get sticky hands from eating. Offer some beverages like coffee or water free with the meal. It's perfectly fine to charge extra for cartons of milk if that is what they want with their pancakes. After they pay, make it easy for your customers by setting up your serving line with plates, utensils, and napkins at the beginning. They are then served two pancakes to start with plus whatever side meat they choose. The customer then moves on to the condiment station where you have plenty of syrup available. These days you probably need to stock some sugar free syrup as well. A lot of your customers will be older and some of them will have problems with their sugar count. Make sure you have plenty of convenient tables with ample seating available. No one wants to eat pancakes standing up. It can be done but it can get very messy. Station plenty of trash cans near the way out and you have just laid out a perfect pancake breakfast.

You will need some people mixing the batter, while someone cooks the pancakes. You will also need some servers to actually place food items on the customer's plates. You don't want the customers helping themselves. Another key to making this successful is that you will want a convenient, well known and safe location. Hopefully you can get the location for a minimal fee or even free. Free is what most organizations go for with a pancake breakfast. Remember that you have to advertise this project just like any other project outlined in this book. Great food at reasonable prices will not work if potential customers don't know what you are doing. Many times you can get the ingredients for your pancake breakfast donated. With all volunteer labor and a free location, you will then score one hundred percent profit from this project. Many clubs I have been around will do this twice a year. These regularly occurring breakfasts are eagerly looked forward to by the local community. Try this project and do it well, and you will have a continuing project that yields several hundred dollars each time you do it. This is a simple project but one that you have to work pretty hard to screw up!

ORGANIZATION EVENT P&L SHEET

Organization_____

Event_____

Date_____Location_____

RECEIPTS:

    Total Admission Tickets Sold @ $_____ Gross Sales_____

    Total Admission Tickets Sold @ $_____ Gross Sales_____

                        TOTAL TICKET GROSS SALES_____

    Other Cash Receipts (Concessions)   _____

    Other Cash Receipts (Raffles)   _____

    Other Cash Receipts   _____

                  TOTAL CASH RECEIPTS FOR EVENT_____

ITEM SOLD: BID AMOUNT:

_____

_____

_____

_____

_____

_____

_____

_____

_____

_____

_____

_____

_____

_____

_____

EXPENSES:
Rent_____
Labor_____
Printing_____
Advertising_____
License_____
Security_____
Raffle items_____
Auctions items_____
_____
_____
_____
_____
_____
_____

                                        TOTAL EXPENSES_____

Total Receipts minus Expenses =   NET PROFIT_____

PROJECT EVALUATION

PROJECT TITLE _____

DATE HELD _____ LOCATION _____

TOTAL REVENUE $_____

TOTAL EXPENSES $_____

NET PROFIT $_____

Problems that should corrected:

_____
_____
_____
_____
_____
_____
_____
_____
_____

Project Summary:

_____
_____
_____
_____
_____
_____
_____
_____
_____

Project Chairperson _____

Signature _____

Date _____

Resource List

Where do I go to buy prizes, insurance, custom t-shirts, tickets or other supplies?

Now that everybody has computer access, even if they have to use the free ones at the public library, finding everything you need to put on your project is a lot easier than it ever was in the past.

Carnival Supplies

To get the most up-to-date information on carnival supplies simply type "carnival prizes" in Google or your personal favorite search engine and see the list. See the list below for some currently active sources.

Oriental Trading Company
P.O. Box 2308
Omaha, NE 68103-2308
www.orientaltrading.com
1-800-875-8480

U.S. Toy Company
www.ustoy.com
1-800-832-0224

Carnival Depot
983 Scott Center Road
Susquehanna, PA 18847
www.carnivaldepot.com
1-570- 461-3000

Small Toys
Novelty House Inc.
50720 Corporate Dr
Shelby Twp., MI 48315
www.smalltoys.com
1-800-633-4477 Ext 14

Carnival Savers
12400 W Highway 71
Suite 350-385
Bee Cave, TX 7873
www.carnivalsavers.com
1-800-507-2985

American Carnival Mart
1317 Lindbergh Plaza Center
Saint Louis, MO 63132-1911
www.funcarnival.com
1-800-991-6818

Akron Novelty Merchandise Company
5240 Wooster Road, W.
Barberton, Ohio 44203
www.akron-novelty.com
1-800-289-8819

CarnivalToys.com
www.carnivaltoys.com
Go to their online site for orders and to see their merchandise displayed. They have live chat for questions on items for sale.

Rhode Island Novelty
www.rinovelty.com
1-800-528-5599

National Prize and Toy Company
www.nationalprizeandtoy.com
1-888-442-8696

Windy City Novelties
www.windycitynovelties.com
1-800-442-9722

Wholesale Party Supplies
www.wholesalepartysupplies.com
1-605-271-7393

Star Track Wholesalers
www.startrackinc.com
1-631-293-6654

Custom T-shirt Printing

To get the most up-to-date information on T-shirt printing simply type "t-shirt printing" in Google or your personal favorite search engine and see the list. See the list below for some currently active sources. Compare prices for the number of shirts you want to purchase. There can be a wide range in prices based on volume and the sizes purchased. Remember to buy sizes that fit your target audience. People are a lot larger than they used to be.

Uberprints.com
www.uberprints.com
1-866-440-8237

Rush Order Tees
www.rushordertees.com
1-800-620-1233

Custom Ink
www.customink.com
1-800-293-4232

Blue Cotton
www.bluecotton.com
1-800-536-1435

Underground Printing
www.undergroundshirts.com
1-800-242-4787

Cafe Press
www.cafepress.com
1-877-809-1659

Poster Printing

To get the most up-to-date information on poster printing simply type "poster printing" in Google or your personal favorite search engine and see the list. See the list below for some currently active sources. Compare prices for the number of posters and sizes you want to purchase. There can be a wide range in prices based on poster size and volume purchased.

U Printing
www.uprinting.com
1-888-888-4211

Print Runner
www.printrunner.com
1-888-296-5760

Vistaprint
www.vistaprint.com
1-866-614-8002

Shortrun Posters
www.shortrunposters.com
1-877-856-0115

Next Day Flyers
www.nextdayflyers.com
1-855-898-9870

Event Insurance

You can usually purchase event insurance from your local insurance agent but if you want to deal with a company that really understands event insurance, then you should deal with a professional event insurance company. To get the most up-to-date information on event insurance simply type "event insurance" in Google or your personal favorite search engine and see the list. I've listed a few here to get you started.

Allied Specialty Insurance
www.alliedspecialty.com
1-800-237-3355

Event Insurance
www.specialeventinsurance.com
1-800-364-2433

Event Helper .com
theeventhelper.com
1-855-493-8368

Event Insurance Now
www.eventinsurancenow.com
1-503-977-5639

Professional Wrestling Organizations

To get the most up-to-date information on local professional wrestling promoters simply type "professional wrestling organizations" in Google or your personal favorite search engine and see the list. One thing you will notice is that most of them have not been in business very long. It is a world in which change is constant and has been so for at least the last thirty five years. For that reason alone, I will not waste the effort to list any of them here. Just use a search engine to find out who is currently in business in your area.

Concert Information

To get the most up-to-date information on available talent simply type "entertainment agencies" in Google or your personal favorite search engine and see the list. See the list below for some currently active sources. There can be a wide range in prices based on the day of the week your show is on and whether your town is on or close to the route the touring act is following.

Schell Shock Entertainment Agency
schellshockentertainmentagency.com
Contact by internet.

Resource Entertainment Group
www.regmemphis.com
1-901-543-1155

Talent Agency Florida
www.williamclare.com
1-727-789-4594

Consultation or Public Speaking

Rick Montana
4791 Dory Circle, Southside, AL 35907
rmontana1@juno.com
Rick Montana/Facebook